The Authors

William Clinkenbeard was born and grew up in Lincoln, Nebraska, USA. He has degrees from the University of Nebraska, McCormick Theological Seminary and Yale Divinity School. His first job was installing Intercontinental Ballistic Missiles during the Cold War. He served as the pastor of Wood River Presbyterian Church in Nebraska and then as the minister of Carrick Knowe Parish Church in Edinburgh. He retired in 2000 after twenty-nine years at Carrick Knowe and spends a lot of his time writing mostly fiction, either in Edinburgh or Arizona.

Ian Gilmour was brought up in Millerston, near Glasgow. He was educated at Clifton High School, Glasgow College of Commerce and Glasgow College of Technology, before graduating with a B.D. from Trinity College, Glasgow. His first parish was Drylaw Parish Church in Edinburgh, and from there he went to serve as minister at South Leith Parish Church. He was a key figure in the Church without Walls Project and became the minister of the newly united St Andrew's and St George's West in Edinburgh in 2010. He is at present the Moderator of Edinburgh Presbytery.

Andrew McLellan was educated at Kilmarnock Academy, Madras College (St Andrews), the University of St Andrews, the University of Glasgow, and Union Theological Seminary. He served as assistant minister at St George's West, the minister of Cartsburn Augustine Church, Greenock, and of Viewfield Parish Church, Stirling. From 1986 until 2002 he was the minister of St Andrew's and St George's Church. He served as the Convener of the Church and Nation Committee from 1992-1996 and as Moderator of the General Assembly in 2000. He also served as Chief Inspector of HM Prisons in Scotland.

Books

By William Clinkenbeard
The Contemporary Lesson, *The Bavelaw Press*
Mind the Gap: Moving between Pulpit and Pew, *The Bavelaw Press*
Ripples Across the Bay (Editor): Fictional Short Stories, *iUniverse*
Writers at Bay (Editor): Fictional Short Stories, *iUniverse*
O is for Oval, Oswald and Osama, a Novel, *iUniverse*
The Battle of Inchcolm Abbey, A Novel, *iUniverse*

By Ian Gilmour (with William Clinkenbeard)
Full on the Eye: Perspectives on the World, The Church, & the Faith, *The Bavelaw Press, 1994*

By Andrew McLellan
Preaching for these People, *Mowbray 1996*
Gentle and Passionate: Reflections from a Year as Moderator (On Reflection), *St Andrew Press, 2001*

THE ONE TREE

A BRIEF THEOLOGICAL HISTORY OF ST ANDREW'S AND ST GEORGE'S WEST, EDINBURGH

William W. Clinkenbeard

Foreword by Ian Y. Gilmour
Recollections by Andrew R.C. McLellan

All profits from the sale of this book go to
St Andrew's and St George's West Church.

All rights reserved. No part of this publication may be reproduced,
stored in a retrieval system, or transmitted in any form by any means,
electronic, mechanical, photocopying, recording or otherwise, without
the prior permission of the publisher.

Published 2013 by Pilrig Press, Edinburgh, Scotland

The right of William Clinkenbeard to be identified as the author
of this work has been asserted by him in accordance with the
Copyright Designs and Patent Act 1988.

All rights reserved.

A CIP catalogue record for this book is available on request from
the British Library.

ISBN 978-0-9566144-6-9

www.pilrigpress.co.uk

Printed in Great Britain by Imprint Digital

Pilrig Press

Acknowledgements

A number of members of St Andrew's and St George's West have provided me with books, pamphlets, leaflets and stories in order to help fill out this story. I want to express my thanks to them for their valuable assistance. I'm sorry if a particularly important aspect of the story to them does not appear herein. Please rest assured that everything did go into the learning mix even if it isn't obvious. My wife Janette always displays amazing patience while the writing process is going on, and her interest goes beyond what is reasonable to extend to reading the manuscript and making helpful suggestions. I know that Donna Gilmour and Irene McLellan have given valuable support to their husbands during the process.

Profuse thanks go to those who have proof-read the manuscript: Lee Young, Janette and John Clinkenbeard in Arizona, Alan and Jean Mackinlay, Ali Pandian, Arthur Chapman, and Desmond Ryan in Edinburgh. I am grateful to them all not only for pointing out typographical mistakes and grammatical errors, but also for correcting some facts. Nevertheless, any remaining errors should be attributed only to the author. Thanks are also due to Peter Wright of *Fuelled Design* for the imaginative cover, to James MacPherson for the majority of the photographs, and to Marc Pimbert of *Pilrig Press* for his helpfulness.

I suspect that a high degree of anxiety grips any author as he or she prepares the final manuscript for the publisher. The printed format is so final and fixed, while our view of history is ever-changing. As the deadline approaches, you become acutely aware of the other ways you could have approached the writing, of what you have omitted and perhaps shouldn't have, of what you included and shouldn't have, and of the folly of attempting the whole thing in the first place. I feel all these things, but I hope that what emerges will be of value to someone.

Finally, my thanks to Ian Gilmour for asking me to undertake what has been a fascinating adventure.

William Clinkenbeard
Fountain Hills, Arizona
March, 2013

St Andrew and St George. The front door handles, 13 George Street

Ministry Team - Ian Gilmour, Ali Pandian and Tony Bryer, Spring 2013

Ministry Team - Ian Gilmour, Ali Pandian and Tony Bryer, Spring 2013

The refurbished George Street building, from the gallery 2013

St Andrew's and St George's after the refurbishment

*The Chapel,
13 George Street*

The chancel at 58 Shandwick Place, formerly St George's West

13 George Street, with the tree in the background

St George's Church, Charlotte Square, now West Register House

The Shandwick Place building (formerly St George's West)

The Dr Alfred Hollins Plaque

The Musical Director, Brigitte Harris and the current choir

One of the 40 Christian Aid Sales at 13 George Street

Dr Robert Candlish, leader of the Free Church

Interior of St Andrew's Church at the Disruption Assembly, from a drawing in the "Illustrated London News," 3rd June 1843

1843 : The Disruption : protesters marching from St. Andrew's Church, George Street, Edinburgh, to Tanfield.

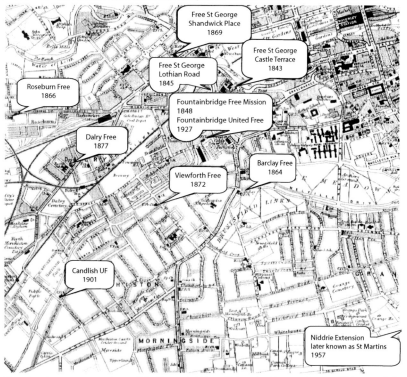

The daughter congregations of St George's West (Printed with permission of Harper Collins)

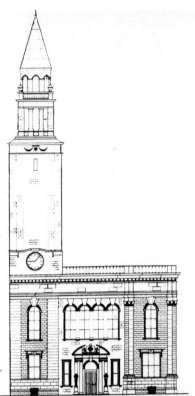

Free St George's, later St George's West

The Tower : built 1879-81

Jiving at Cephas, in a very imaginative youth programme

Contents

Introduction

When Ian Gilmour asked me to write a history of St Andrew's and St George's West Church, I wasn't sure. I normally write fiction these days, and I'm not a historian. However, it eventually became clear that what was wanted was more akin to a theological history of these two churches, now united as one. It was to be an attempt to pin-point some of the significant events in their histories in order to comprehend their union and give shape to the future. Ian and I wrote a book together way back in 1994. Called *Full on the Eye: Perspectives on the world, the Church and the Faith*, it dealt with what we felt were the significant theological and ecclesiastical issues of the day. The book didn't make much impact upon the church or the world. However, we have always felt that *Full on the Eye* raised a number of significant issues, and that it would be worthwhile looking at these points again in the light of the passage of time. So several of the theological issues we explored do resurface in this work. Perhaps the most important of these is what shape the church ought to have in the future.

This book could not be called a *history* in the strict sense. I have used secondary sources rather than primary sources for the most part. A thorough-going history would demand that the session records of the churches for over two hundred years be studied, and I couldn't do that. I have tried to analyse the leadership styles of a number of ministers of these congregations, but this has proved a rather selective process, mainly because of the absence of material. Some readers will no doubt be disappointed when they are unable to find extensive coverage of their favourite minister. Moreover, while there is at least some source material about the work of ministers, there is very little about the efforts of loyal elders and members. I regret that in this book they may be neglected. Nevertheless, I want to emphasise that this is not intended to be a comprehensive historical study of the churches, but rather a theological analysis of certain key points in a long history.

But if this work was not strictly going to be a history, what was it? I struggled with the question for a long time. I didn't want it to be a rather objective and perhaps somewhat tedious record of historical development, but more of a tool, a way of informing the members and others connected with the church about the whole fascinating sweep of the past in order to equip them for their future as a new church. So the work finally took on the shape of a handbook, a kind of pocket guide which said:

These are some of the facts that lie in your long history as churches; in here you will observe some of the shoulders of heroes on which you now stand; here are some of the turning points where your predecessors saw things correctly and made good decisions; here are some issues where they did not see clearly and made bad decisions; these are some of the myths about the past which need to be dispelled.

When he was writing to the young churches, St Paul addressed his letters to *The Saints* in the various cities, Corinth, Colossae, and Rome. So I had no hesitation in thinking of this book as a kind of handbook for the *Saints in St Andrew's and St George's West Church in Edinburgh*. To be honest, I haven't heard of such a book being produced before, so I am conscious of perhaps breaking new ground. If that is so, then I'm sure that I have made many mistakes in the ploughing.

The exercise has been fascinating. Two hundred and fifty years ago Edinburgh was confined to a narrow and rocky ridge, but it was the intellectual capital of the world. A New Town was planned and built, and two new churches were planted within it. Over many years and amidst many changes, these churches have made a major impact upon the world. That's the story, and it's a good one. In the *Foreword* we will hear first from the minister of St Andrew's and St George's West, The Reverend Ian Y. Gilmour. What are his hopes and intentions in a demanding situation? In the *Recollection* we shall hear from a person uniquely qualified to reflect on his experience in both churches, The Very Reverend Andrew McClellan, who served as Assistant Minister in St George's West and then as Minister in St Andrew's and St George's. On with the story.

Foreword

By The Reverend Ian Y. Gilmour

I am most grateful to Bill Clinkenbeard and Andrew McLellan. They are excellent writers and I really appreciate their labour on this stimulating book.

It was my hope, when I asked Bill to write this book, that it would help all those interested to appreciate that this story has local, national, and international dimensions. I hoped it would be a thoughtful and a challenging book. I hoped it would put some flesh upon the great figures in the story, so that readers could better understand them and the context for their work. I hoped it would invite some new thoughts regarding our congregation, the Church of Scotland and indeed the whole church. I honestly believe it surpasses my hopes.

Bill tells the story of the development of the New Town within Scotland's capital, the great city of Edinburgh. He skilfully weaves through that tale, the unique story of the dismembering and then grafting back together of a congregation and a denomination. He does this with imagination and wisdom.

Andrew has shared personal insights in his strong connection with each of these congregations. His generous and thoughtful contribution both expands and personalises some of the points made in the text.

Bill, Andrew and I are fortunate to share three things in common:

- *We have all studied at Glasgow University.*
- *We have each served as moderator of Edinburgh presbytery.*
- *We have outstanding 'better' halves who all come from the west of Scotland in Janette, Irene and Donna.*

I hope the end result of reading this book might be for you not only to gain new insights into a congregation, but might also allow you to think more deeply about your own faith story, the beliefs and the experiences which have shaped you and also the city or community in which you live. Finally, I hope some readers will be inspired to do at least one of the following: *Think a new thought, work harder for your community, support the needy, give glory to God, follow the way of Jesus and serve His Body on earth, the Christian Church. None of these goals is particularly popular in our culture during this era; however, they remain vital for our health as individuals and as a community, society and country.*

I begin with the words of a young woman: Ali Pandian, who wrote this prayerful poem for the congregation. She is a student minister and she read it at our last service in the Shandwick Place building, formerly St George's West.

Travelling On

The time has arrived for us to move home
Not to dwindle or wander or to endlessly roam
We're on a new path with God as our guide
Our shepherd from behind and our companion beside.
And all are invited, and all have a space
For each individual there's a cherished place
So we travel on, journey forward together
Travelling with a purpose, to God will we tether.

But how will we get there? I hear you wonder
With a flash of light or a rumble of thunder?
Some may plod with a weary load and a backward glance
Some may run, some skip, some eagerly dance
Some tiptoe, cautious of what lies ahead
Some lead with their heart, some lead with their head
Some on sticks, some on wheels
Some wearing high heels
And all are invited, and all have a space
For each individual there's a cherished place
So we travel on, journey forward together
Travelling with a purpose, to God will we tether.

And what will we take? I hear you enquire
All the things that a heart could desire?
We take words from our Maker and prayers on our lips
We take unity and friendship and vision that grips
We take hearts full of promise, and eyes looking about
Hands that love working and reaching out
We take singers and thinkers and bakers and more

We take those who bring welcome and an open door
And all are invited, and all have a space
For each individual there's a cherished place
So we travel on, journey forward together
Travelling with a purpose, to God will we tether.

Ali Pandian, February 2013

Moving onwards does seem a good motif for our congregation in its third year of incarnation as St Andrew's and St George's West. As I write, in March 2013, the Shandwick Place building was sold to Charlotte Baptist Church on the first day of the month. Further, they asked three representatives to participate in their first service in the building on Sunday 17 March. It was in one sense the finale to a bold chapter in both the life of the Free Presbyterian Church and the Church of Scotland, a chapter which lasted 170 years and which touched people on every continent. That chapter has now been concluded, but this is not a time to be despondent. T.S. Eliot suggests, *"What we call the beginning is often the end. And to make an end is to make a beginning."* He also suggests, *"Only those who risk going too far can possibly find out how far one can go."* I would like to set this sentiment alongside the comforting words of Jesus, *"**I will be with you always.**"* Jesus does promise to be with us, but that should not be a reason to sit back and wallow, enjoying His presence. His example is of purposeful activity, moving on, challenging religious leaders, encouraging new converts, speaking forcefully and healing even those who grab at his garments. His call is simple: *"**Follow Me.**"* His story is dynamite: just read Mark's gospel for yourself.

The Body of Christ

The body of Christ is the most important metaphor for the church and it is a tremendously helpful one. Paul, the New Testament leader and letter writer, uses it more than once in his famous letters. He reminds his readers that working together is crucial, for we are designed to be interdependent.

"Christ is like a single body, which has many parts; it is still one body, even though it is made up of different parts ... And so there is no division in the body, but all its different parts have the same concern for one another. If one part of the body suffers, all the other parts suffer with it; if one part is praised, all the other parts share its happiness." (1 Cor. 12)

Missing Parts?

When we read any historical text we should keep an open ear, listening for whom or what is missing. So in this history there are many missing groups – children, women, black people, young people, gay people, common or garden church members, elders and people of other faiths. In other words, most church history focuses on a tiny percentage of the human species speaking to and about God in public. It can be argued that the main characters in this story, nearly all males, play the part of ecclesiastical entertainers in the limelight of premier pulpits. Further, in more recent years it has become clear how difficult it is to effect change in the church. We need to move out from the mindset of *church* as an image of steeple and male minister who issues pulpit wisdom out to members as passive receivers who are asked only to listen and follow like sheep.

You will make up your own mind on this, but if it is true, then theologically it contradicts the teachings of Jesus: *"Let the children come to me..."* and Paul: *"In Christ Jesus you are all one, no more male or female, black or white ..."* and Luther's main focus at the Reformation: the *"Priesthood of all Believers".*

These three great leaders take inclusive positions and are keen to share ministry widely and to connect with people from every age-band and background. It is not that the ministers described here were wrong or less than fully committed. In fact, all the ministers in these congregations contributed well and were widely recognised to be gifted by the wider church and community. Some did strive to alter the popular mindsets.

Jesus dynamically calls humble working people and invites them into his way of working, then sends them out to learn through their own experience. Paul never has a building, but adapts quickly to the cultural context in which he finds himself. Martin Luther works and fights for the Bible to be translated into the common language of each country so that it can reshape people's lives, and thus encourage independent relationships with God which are not dependent on a priestly intermediary.

So as you read *One Tree*, learn from the successes and failures of those who play their parts in a stimulating and rich story. Please switch on your radar as you read for those whose voices are not heard and who are missing from the key scenes. For in so doing you may be able to discern a new pathway ahead for

St Andrew's and St George's West and even for the Church of Scotland.

I believe the church needs the wisdom of how to nurture believers into mature human beings who will help to create a strong community identity. It certainly needs people who take scripture seriously, people who love both their neighbours and their enemies, people who behave like the Christ as well as follow his teaching, people who use all the creative energy of the church to affect the world in many positive ways. Does this chime with the teaching of Luther, Paul and Jesus?

What will the church look like in fifty years? I can't be certain, but I do know that if it is to regain the focus, vigour and impact of its early days, it will need to regain its direction by learning from Jesus, Paul and Luther in that order.

What is a Local Congregation for?

In the late 1980s this helpful summary was offered by St Andrew's and St George's:

We believe God's purpose for the congregation is to love and glorify God and spread the good news joyfully. To seek to pursue God's purpose enthusiastically and attractively.

*We believe that it is fundamental to our purposes to be outward looking; and our strategies will encourage all the members of the congregation to share in the **ministries** and the **leadership**.*

A Way Ahead

It is an excellent statement which can be used as a benchmark, and it echoes Paul's superb metaphor: *"All of you are Christ's body, and each one is a part of it."*

If this statement were to be scrupulously applied, evaluated and reviewed, it could change any congregation for the better. In too many congregations we are good at finding helpful ideas month by month at our meetings, but never implementing them, nor testing them rigorously.

I believe that St Andrew's and St George's West can grow if we:

a) **root** ourselves firmly in the gifts of God the Creator who is source of life, energy and renewal.

b) form key supporters into a **trunk**. God has given gifts for the building up of His body.

c) change the patterns of **formation** for leaders, with more opportunities being offered, both for professional ministers in paid positions and for novices to be encouraged/expected to undergo life-long training, if the tree is to flourish fully.

d) **branch** out through children and the less confident adults after they have been enabled to 'discover their voice' and their ministry.

e) **grow,** *when the key people are*
   growing *individually in knowledge and*
   love. Genuine growth can take place
   in congregations. This growth will be
   measured numerically, but also through
   atmosphere, depth of thinking, the ability
   to challenge worldly standards, while
   adapting to the environment.

f) *are open to new ideas, new people,*
   those from other faiths and other
   denominations, so important for healthy
   budding, flowering *and* ***fruiting.***

In the Bible, trees are commended for offering shelter, shade and sanctuary, giving us food and providing new perspectives, while contributing building material and creating warmth. They are present from the beginning to the end of the biblical account, from the Garden of Eden to the last chapter of Revelation. They journey with us theologically, though sometimes we simply cannot see the wood for them! Trees usually outlive us and thus they are often used as a symbol of, or metaphor for, stability, reliability and continuity.

One single tree is the logo of St Andrew's and St George's West, based on the only tree in George Street. It can serve as a reminder to root the congregation in God's Word, while stretching upwards and outwards, ever working and worshipping to bring glory to God. The next stage is for the congregation to be a seeding station for more trees, which root, shoot and flourish, revealing the loving purpose of the Maker of all.

I started with a non-minister's contribution and will deliberately finish with another, an excellent, thoughtful prayer from one of the current elders at St Andrew's and St George's West, Arthur Chapman. I hope it serves to highlight the reservoir of talent in elders and members which is hidden in too many congregations.

A Prayer for St Andrew's & St George's West

O God,
source of all being,
we pray for your church
in this place at this time.
Grant that we may be blessed with renewed strength, faith, and love.
May we discern your will and so enable your purpose to be shown
in all we say and do.
Help us to find new ways
to bring your good news
of abundant living
and wasteful loving
to the communities around us.
Let your spirit of love and peace,
hospitality and honesty,
community and challenge
dwell among us.
Grant that this place
may continue to be a place
of love to the loveless,
hope to the hopeless,
and celebration and joy to
the downhearted and depressed.
May the light of your love,
The peace of Jesus Christ and
the fellowship of the Holy Spirit shine
out to inform and illuminate our world. Amen

At a personal level, it is a great pleasure and a considerable responsibility to serve the city centre in Edinburgh, to work with so many talented people, and be called to seek new paths into hearts, minds and lives in the name of love.

Ian Y Gilmour,
Minister, St Andrew's and St George's West,
March 2013

CHAPTER I

Life on the Ridge

There is a solitary tree standing outside a church on George Street in Edinburgh. It provides us with a useful image of the Christian Church in the world. If we think of Christianity as having its roots in the Old and New Testaments and the early church, the trunk could then be seen as the whole church in the world. There are many larger and smaller limbs, several of which are in Scotland. In the course of history one limb has produced a number of branches, due mainly to developments in the nineteenth century. Now, two of these branches of the Church of Scotland, formerly separated, have been bound together into one very significant part of the living tree. It's called St Andrew's and St George's West. This new union of two churches has a fascinating history which we try to illuminate in this little book.

From an intellectual point of view Edinburgh occupies a unique place in history; John Buchan can write the following: *"For a period of nearly half a century, from about the time of the Highland rebellion of 1754 until the French Revolution of 1789, the small city of Edinburgh ruled the western intellect.*

For nearly fifty years, a city that had for centuries been a byword for poverty, religious bigotry, violence and squalor laid the mental foundations for the modern world".[1]

Two churches, St Andrew's and St George's, planted early in Edinburgh's New Town, played a unique role in helping to shape the city's part in laying such foundations. These two historic churches have now become one: St Andrew's and St George's West. This book is an attempt to explore the background and development of this church over the years. For any real understanding of the history of this church in Edinburgh's New Town it is essential to acquire a historical image of Edinburgh's Old Town. Yet for those who know present-day Edinburgh it is very difficult to visualise the city of old, severely limited by both its geography and its history of hostile attack from outside. This is because today there is a continuity of city landscape that was not there three hundred years ago. Some imagination is therefore required in order to gain such an image. So an appeal to the reader: imagine yourself as an ageless observer standing on the esplanade leading to Edinburgh Castle. To the west your view is limited by the castle, but you enjoy a good downward view to the north, the east, and the south. Underneath the tarmac on which you stand is the granite plug of an ancient volcano at the high point of a ridge running east for a mile. On both sides of the ridge are deep depressions formed by the gougings of an ice-age glacier. From this vantage point you are able to observe the changes around you as they take place through the centuries. In the second century AD you might just be able to make out Roman forts to the west and east, at Cramond and Inveresk, with the Antonine Wall running west from

[1] John Buchan, *Capital of the Mind, How Edinburgh Changed the world*, p.1

Cramond towards Stirling. By the middle of the eighth century you watch as Edinburgh is put under siege, and the hill fort/castle comes under the control of the Anglo-Saxon kingdom of Northumbria. In the middle of the ninth century you watch the first St Giles', a Roman Catholic church, being built just down the road. You see Malcolm III refortify the castle and the town during the eleventh century. Then in 1125 you watch as David I founds the burgh or town, and three years later Holyrood Abbey. In the middle of the sixteenth century you witness John Knox being appointed as the Presbyterian minister of St Giles', and watch as the Scottish Reformation transforms the country in 1560. You are impressed that in 1561 St Giles', foreshadowing modernity, is a multi-purpose building. In addition to housing a Presbyterian church it contains law courts, a school, the town clerk's office, a prison and work-house. Towards the end of the sixteenth century you note that Edinburgh now has about a dozen ministers and that the commerce of the town is booming. There are five hundred merchants and five hundred craftsmen in the city, of which two hundred and fifty are tailors. There are two hundred and eighty-eight brewers or alewives in the town. By the end of the seventeenth century you note that the town has its first coffeehouse, the first regular stagecoaches to London and Glasgow and that the professional classes outnumber the merchants. There are two hundred lawyers or writers, twenty-four surgeons and thirty-three physicians. These professionals are waited upon by over five thousand domestic servants. Edinburgh is growing fast.

When it comes to the middle of the eighteenth century you decide to stretch your legs and carry out a little survey on foot. You know already that Edinburgh is a narrow, irregular town jammed onto that ridge, which drops gradually from the castle down to Holyrood Abbey. The first section of the main street of this town is now known as the Lawnmarket and the second section as the Royal Mile. The street is lined by and closed in by high tenements and cluttered by as many as fifteen street markets. Like many European cities it has a herringbone pattern: one long main street intersected by short side streets, narrow passage-ways, and closes. Unlike other cities, however, the tenements soar as high as seven storeys, higher than anywhere else in Europe. The tenements and the hanging smoke from their coal fires act like a curtain and shut out the sun. In the high tenements the wealthy live on the first several levels and the poorer folk above. In a nice turn of phrase, John Buchan writes that "the dark scale-stairs were upright streets, a thoroughfare of Musselburgh fishwives, sweeps or coal-porters and barefoot housemaids."[2]

Walking up or down the Royal Mile takes some care. You have to negotiate very carefully, continuously looking up and down and around. You must look around to avoid horses and carriages thundering up on the cobblestones of the narrow street, up to avoid the waste from chamber pots thrown from tenement windows to the warning cry of Gardyloo ("Watch out for the slop!"), and down to avoid the waste already on the ground. If you turn to the north, you face the deep depression containing the Nor Loch, polluted by the same waste draining down into it and by the tanners on the north side as they use the water in their work. If you turn to the south you face another deep depression, beyond which is marshland. Down in this valley lies the Grassmarket, where horses and cattle are sold and animals are slaughtered. The gallows are down there as well. Beyond the Grassmarket lies the city wall, protecting

[2] *Buchan, p.6*

the south and east approaches to the city, while the castle rock and the Nor Loch protect the north and west. Your survey confirms your guess about why the city rose up vertically rather than spread out horizontally. The ridge constrained the town geographically, and fear made the residents wary of going beyond the city walls. Estimates of the population in these days vary, but there might have been as many as forty to fifty thousand people living in very cramped, airless and dirty conditions. These confined circumstances meant that the residents of every rank and station shared the same public spaces. There certainly was community, perhaps too much of it, because the inhabitants encountered each other everywhere they went: in the corridors and on the stairs of their houses, in the closes, in the churches and institutions, on the narrow pavements with their markets along the High Street, and in shops and pubs. There were very few public buildings, so meetings often had to be held in pubs, which created obvious problems for town sobriety. Lots of business and conversation was done outside, often at the Mercat Cross, just down from St Giles'. Certainly there was a vibrant life on the ridge, but the town looked bad and smelled worse and disease was taking its toll. In 1619 the Privy Council had ordered the burgh to clean up its streets. In 1751 a survey found severe dilapidation in the city.

Beyond the narrow confines of the ridge there were pleasant pastoral scenes: a river running from the southern hills to the Firth of Forth, some woods and more hills, and tucked away between them some little settlements. Lying in the shadow of the castle was St Cuthbert's Church. Miles beyond that was a ring of villages and churches at Cramond, Gogar, Corstorphine, Ratho, Dalmeny, Abercorn, Currie, Hailes,

Liberton, and Duddingston. To the northeast was Leith, the major port for Edinburgh and Europe's gateway into the city. It was from Leith that Edinburgh received most of its supplies: its glass and soap, wine and whisky. From there, and from nearly all of the surrounding villages, Edinburgh could be spotted by the clouds of smoke from a thousand coal fires rising above its tenements.

You visit St Giles', where there had been a church on the site from the middle of the ninth century, but the history of that church until the sixteenth century is uncertain and complicated. You find that in 1150 it had a priest and a grange, or home-farm. In 1393 it was granted to the Abbey of Scone. The first known vicar was named John, mentioned in 1241. It suffered from raids and burnings by the English. At the time of the Reformation in Scotland in 1560, St Giles' was a collegiate church. The structure was divided into four: Trinity College, serving the northeast of the burgh; Old or Great St Giles', serving the southeast; Upper Tollbooth, the southwest; and Mew or East, Little or High, serving the northwest. Two ministers were assigned to each church. Between St Giles' and the outlying ring of churches, the parish belonged to St Cuthbert's. Canongate, a separate burgh down the Royal Mile, used the church of Holyrood-House for worship.[3]

On your little survey you find that life on the ridge is humming and good at least for some, but not so good for many others. The overcrowded space is imposing too many problems. You come to the end of your little walk feeling slightly suffocated, thinking that something has to give. Some new space was required for the town, and the new space that Edinburgh got changed things forever.

[3] Ian Dunlop, *The Kirks of Edinburgh*, Scottish Records Society, 1988, p.54

CHAPTER 2

Life on Stately Streets

B y the middle of the eighteenth century there was pressure on the town council to do something to ease the problems of the Old Town. The thinking behind the pressure was both negative and positive. Something had to be done to ease the overcrowding and the bad conditions, but the town council also wanted to attract some of the wealthier people back to the town from London and elsewhere. The ideal man of the times turned out to be Provost George Drummond. George Drummond had been born in Blairgowrie and attended the High School in Edinburgh. He was an accountant and had been six times elected to the town council. He had raised money to construct the Royal Infirmary and had supported the enlargement of the University of Edinburgh. Intent on doing something to improve the conditions of the Old Town, he first succeeded in having the Royal Burgh extended northwards, to the area beyond the nasty and inconvenient Nor Loch. Then in 1766 he persuaded the council to set a competition to find a design for this new area. There is nothing to indicate how easy or difficult it was to convince the town council, but one might imagine that it took some effort.

Drummond's success in persuading the council to create a new area for the town is the first of what might be called turning points. His perception of the needs of a growing community, plus his vision of its expansion, plus his courage in pursuing the matter changed the shape of Edinburgh. Throughout this book we shall be attempting to highlight a number of such turning points.

The competition was entered by James Craig, an apprentice mason who was only twenty-six years old at the time. Craig set about his work, and it must have been exhilarating to sit down with paper and pen in order to design a new town. Nothing quite like this had been tried before. Sadly, George Drummond died before the competition was completed, so Craig's design went to Drummond's successor, Provost Gilbert Laurie, in 1767. The plan proposed three main east-west streets and seven north-south streets, forming a grid system with a large square at each end of the central east-west street. Between the east-west streets were narrow streets or lanes with mews for servants, stables and carriages. The plan is inscribed to "His Sacred Majesty George III, whose people enjoy the peace, security and liberty under his mild and auspicious government." Craig proposed giving royal names to the streets as an expression of loyalty to the union between Scotland and England. Thus, in honour of the patron saints of the two countries, it was to be St Andrew's Square (now St Andrew Square) and St George's Square. However, George Square already existed on the south side of the town, so to avoid confusion the name was changed to Charlotte Square, after the queen. The southernmost street was to be St Giles' Street, after Scotland's patron saint. This was rejected by the king because it was the name of the patron saint of lepers and also a slum area near London. The street became *Princes Street* after George's sons. *Frederick Street* was named after the king's father and *Hanover Street* after the family name. The lanes were named after England's national emblem (*Rose Street*), and after Scotland's national emblem (*Thistle Street*). Today, Craig's plan looks rather simple, but after a modification which removed controversial diagonal streets that were intended to suggest the union flag, Craig's plan won the competition and he was awarded the Freedom of the City.

On James Craig's original drawing there is also a cartouche enclosing part of a poem written by his uncle James Thomson. Thomson was born in Ednam in 1700, the son of a Presbyterian minister. Thomson would become a popular poet of the day, providing among other things the words for the patriotic piece *Rule Britannia*. Yet he was apparently undistinguished at school. His headmaster considered him to be "without a common share of parts." Nevertheless, James Craig thought enough of his uncle to quote these lines from Thomson's poem Liberty on his drawing:

> AUGUST, around, what PUBLIC WORKS I see!
> Lo! Stately Streets, lo! Squares that Court the breeze,
> See! long canals, and deepened Rivers join
> Each part with each, and with the circling Main,
> The whole enliven'd Isle.

James Craig's plan for a new town is another turning point in our story, for there are on his plan only two designated sites, both for churches, named by him as *St Andrew's and St George's*. The fact that he quotes his uncle's poem and that

James Thomson was the son of a Presbyterian minister has to be regarded as significant. A critic writing in *Poetry Foundation* suggests that the poem *Liberty* was a cry against selfishness, party politics, luxury and despotism. Thomson, he says, wanted the state "to belong to all rather than simply to the king, and not be an arena for self-interest."[4] It's possible that Craig was ideologically moved by such sentiment, but taking into account his age, the circumstances, and the inscription to the king, it is equally likely that he was aesthetically moved by the vision produced by the poem's second line: *Stately Streets, Squares that Court the breeze.* Whatever the case it is clear that St Andrew's and St George's churches must in large part owe their existence to James Craig.

It is important to study Craig's plan in more detail. In contrast to plans drawn for other cities round about the same time, this proposal appears very plain and modest. Surely, we might say today, this idea is too simple. It is only a grid system, comprised of three streets running one way and seven streets the other way, along with two large squares. The diagonal streets which in the first plan would have added some variation have been deleted. Does the new space not seem like a rectangular void? Yet the design must be seen in relation to the nature of the Old Town. These are wide, straight streets, George Street being eighty feet in width, with walkways of ten feet on each side for pedestrians. Where was anything like that in the Old Town? St Andrew's and Charlotte Squares feature large, light, open spaces. Where in the Old Town was anything like that? Rose and Thistle Streets, while narrow, have lanes with mews to permit stables and quarters for

---

[4] *"James Thomson", in Poetry Foundation*

servants. Where were such things in the Old Town? Surely, in the light of the horrendous conditions of the Old Town, Craig has indeed created stately streets and squares that court the breeze. Trees appear on the plan beyond Princes Street and Queen Street. Where were the trees of the Old Town? What appears modest to us now surely was, in the eighteenth century, quite radical.

Craig placed his two churches at the focal points of the squares at each end of George Street. Visually, these were the ideal locations. Would he have included the churches if his uncle had not been the son of a Presbyterian minister? The other sites were for houses and shops. Work on the New Town began in 1767, a remarkably short lead time for such a large project. After the experience in the Old Town, sanitation had obviously been made a priority. Craig himself was sent to London to learn how to construct sewers, as no one in Edinburgh knew how to build them. As excavations were made for buildings, the extracted material was used to make the Mound, which when completed in 1781, allowed the Nor Loch to be skirted. A few years later it would be drained to create a park, now called *Princes Street Gardens*. Again, this was thanks to Provost George Drummond. The far-seeing and progressive provost also proposed the North Bridge, which bridged the depression and would permit much easier access to Leith and the country north of Queen Street.

In Craig's design the buildings along the three east-west streets were to be residential, while those on the north-south streets were to be for shops. The town council would determine how the plots were to be sold and their prices, along with the number of storeys permitted and the width of pavements, etc.

Initially, however, sales did not go very well. The plots that the council had marked out were slow to be taken up. After a year, the council had taken in only £972 14s. 7d from the sale of plots.[5] One of the reasons for poor sales must have been the cost of the new houses. To build a house in St Andrew Square would cost you from £1,800 to £2,000. Converting that sum to the 2012 equivalent amounts (conservatively) to £195,000. But there were other reasons as well. For many of the wealthier folk, George Square south of the Cowgate and near the university was still regarded as the best place to live. Moreover, many potential customers must have questioned what life would be like in the New Town. Would you, if you were used to meeting folk on your evening perambulations on the High Street, actually see anyone you knew on the new George Street? And if you lived in the New Town did it not seem a long and cumbersome way to go, around the Nor Loch and up the Mound to the places where most life was lived: the courts, the Kirk, and the markets of the Old Town? So there was no great rush into the unknown spaces of the New Town.

[5] *Buchan, p.197.*

CHAPTER 3

St Andrew's Church: 1781-1843

Things were moving in the New Town, but very slowly. The council offered a premium of £20 to the first person who would build in the New Town. A Mr. John Young built a house close to George Street and got the reward. Another reward of real value (no council taxes) was given to someone for building a house on Princes Street. Gradually, some courageous souls were ready to make the move. David Hume, by now highly respected in the philosophical world and internationally known, bought a small plot for a house at the corner of St Andrew Square and St David Street. And there, in the year 1771, Benjamin Franklin stayed with Hume for a fortnight, a stay which he said gave him the "densest" of pleasures. Franklin's visit to David Hume in Edinburgh underlines the assertion of Edinburgh's position as intellectual capital of the world. On his way to Edinburgh Franklin had reason to stay at what is now Prestonfield House Hotel on the south side. Clearly he enjoyed his stay, for he penned a poem for the proprietors:

Joys of Prestonfield, adieu!
Late found, soon lost, but still we'll view
Th'engaging scene—oft to these eyes
Shall the pleasing vision rise.
Hearts that warm towards a friend,
Kindness on kindness without end,
Easy converse, sprightly wit,
These we found in dame and knight.
Cheerful meals, balmy rest,
Beds that never bugs molest,
Neatness and sweetness all around
These—at Prestonfield we found.
Hear, O Heaven! A stranger's prayer!
Bless the hospitable pair!
Bless the sweet bairns, and very soon
Give these a brother, those a son![6]

Slowly, plots were being purchased and houses erected. It was mainly the professional class who had the money to make the move. But there was a downside to the growth of the New Town. As the stately streets began to flourish and the courtly breezes blew, the Old Town began to become a slum. In 1772, the construction of the North Bridge was completed, allowing for easier travel to and from Leith. In 1775 the estimated population of Edinburgh was fifty-seven thousand, and a directory of the city's brothels and prostitutes was published. By 1780 St Andrews' Square and some parts of Princes Street had been built. James F. Hunter Blair proposed to the council that it was time that the New Town have a place of worship.

[6] *Kindly supplied by the manager of Prestonfield House*

Note that this is the town or city taking the initiative to provide a church for the people. Such churches were known as "burgh churches". James Craig had, of course, already drawn in two churches, one in the commanding place of each square. James Hunter Blair's proposal was agreed in January of 1781, and Blair later became Lord Provost. St Andrew's Church should have gone into its square of the same name. However, Sir Laurence Dundas got in first and purchased the site for his mansion on the square. St Andrew's Church then took charge of a site on the north side of George Street, across from the Royal College of Physicians, a structure which was later taken down.

Clearly, councils in those days believed in offering "prizes for plans", for the town council was then prepared to offer ten guineas for the best plan for the new church. It was to be seventy to eighty feet at the front and sixty to eighty feet in depth and to seat fifteen hundred people. The competition was won by Andrew Frazer (or Fraser) FRSE. Frazer was a soldier and engineer who had been involved with the design and construction of Fort George, and was later partly responsible for the demolition of the port of Dunkirk. Frazer designed an oval church for the council, reportedly the first in Great Britain. It is not clear if the oval design was his own or if he got the idea from somewhere else. The foundation stone was laid on March 21, 1781 and the church completed in 1783. In all, the church cost the council £7,000, £3,000 of which was borrowed from Heriot's Hospital, secured on ale duty. Three years after the church was completed a spire of 168 feet was erected, designed by William Sibbald.

In 1784 the church was sufficiently furnished to advertise for public inspections to take place. This, in turn, permitted applications for sittings. The price of seats varied in relation to where they were and the view of the preacher they afforded. Seat rents might be as much as £64 16s. (Scots), which in today's terms would be approximately £506 (Sterling). However, some seat holders got their seats free. These included the minister, the Lords of Session, the Lord Provost and Magistrates and Major Frazer. Some seat holders could afford to purchase seats for their servants, often in the gallery of the church. There was a book to record the payments of each seat-holder. Seat rents would prove to create some disputes or problems, and we shall hear more about that later on.

Mr. John Young, who won the prize for the first house in the New Town came to the church's aid in respect of a session-house. Mr. Young sent a letter to the Lord Provost, offering to construct on his own land a session-house for the church, fourteen feet square and ten feet high. The council accepted Mr. Young's offer, and they indicated that Mr. Young and his heirs should receive seat No. 80 in return. Now it happened that Seat No. 80 had already been rented by George Ferguson, Advocate. Mr. Ferguson was, however, not to be removed from his seat until another had been provided. It is not indicated if Mr. Ferguson was unhappy about being so ejected.

A chime of six bells was added to the church in 1789 at the cost of £389 10s. A visitor to the church, writing in the *Farrington Diary*, expresses surprise at hearing the bells in Edinburgh. He had understood that the musical ringing of bells was a remnant of Catholicism. Of more interest is that he considered that while George Street was spacious, it was "not compleat." The houses, he believed, were not tall enough for the width of the street. Too many roofs were seen. In walking across the road he found it to be thirty-seven paces wide. The comparison with the streets and roofs of the Old Town is unavoidable.

The ringing of the bells was to cause another problem, albeit much later on in 1836. Someone made a complaint to the Kirk Session that the bell ringers were in the habit, after finishing their bell ringing on Sunday, to repair to a public house, where they spent the rest of the Sabbath drinking. This had been reported to the police, who had sent a sergeant to the pub to investigate. The pub's landlord denied that there were any persons in the house. But upon examining another room above the stairs the sergeant found "six persons, and a woman sitting with spirits before them."[7] This was reported back to the Kirk Session, who in turn sent a copy of the minutes to the Town Council, who alone had the rights to appoint or dismiss the bell ringers.

The first minister of St Andrew's was William Greenfield, called from Wemyss in 1784. Greenfield also served as Professor of Rhetoric at Edinburgh University, this being one of the first chairs of English Literature in the world. After three years, in 1787, he moved to the High Kirk to become the associate of The Reverend Hugh Blair. Blair was a popular preacher, but the poet Robert Burns found William Greenfield better:

"Mr. Greenfield is of a superior order. The bleedings of humanity, the generous resolve, a manly disregard of the paltry subjects of vanity, virgin modesty, the truest taste, and a very sound

---

[7] George Christie, The Story of St Andrew's, Edinburgh, 1934, pp.37-39

judgement characterise him. He being the very first Speaker I ever heard is perhaps half owing to his industry. He certainly possesses no small share of poetic abilities; he is a steady, a most disinterested friend, without the least affectation, of seeming so; and as a companion, his god[?] sense, his joyous hilarity, his sweetness of manners and modesty, are most engagingly charming."[8]

Greenfield became Moderator of the General Assembly and received a Doctorate of Divinity from Edinburgh University. Yet due to some scandal he was stripped of his honour two years later, fled the country and was excommunicated by the church.

By 1785 there was already quite an extensive organisation at St Andrew's. Of the elders on the Kirk Session, four were lawyers and three were doctors, and during the early years lawyers clearly dominated the leadership of the church. But lawyers were not always to everyone's taste. In his autobiography, Benjamin Franklin recalls a letter he sent to Lord Kames: "Persons of good sense ... rarely fall into [disputation] except lawyers, University Men, Men of all Sorts that have been bred in Edinburgh."[9]

Early on in the life of the church there were numerous committees: *Organ and Psalmody, Work Society, Mothers' Meeting, Soup Kitchen, Parochial Association, Sabbath School, Young Men's Fellowship*, and the parish *Literary Society*. And there was a choir of twenty-four, four of whom were professionals. From 1784 onwards worship was led by a Precentor alone or by the choir, but in 1880 an organ would be

---

[8] *"The Reverend William Greenfield", The Burns Encyclopaedia*
[9] *Buchan, p.341, footnote 5*

installed at the cost of £860. A part of the parish of St Cuthbert's was detached from that church and given to St Andrew's in 1787.

During the French Revolution and the Napoleonic Wars a number of military references appear in the records of the church, noting in part the many military weddings which took place there. Between 1815 and 1820 the minister had an average of about sixty weddings per year. The collection or offering on April 18, 1818 was £159 9s. (sterling), but foreign coins or "bad money" were also often found in the collection. In the record of collections, comments were often made about the level of the offering in relation to bad weather, confirming that nothing much changes! In these days there were normally twelve elders on the Kirk Session, and they met six to eight times a year. One interesting practice took place in respect of communion. It lasted four days, beginning with a preparatory service on Thursday evening and concluding with dinner for the Kirk Session on Monday.

A Sunday School for children was started in 1812 and a day school for poor children after that. Alexander McLean, a perfumer and hairdresser in the New Town, left £1000 to found a parish school. In 1858 a property was purchased on Thistle Street to furnish a chapel providing worship services to poorer people. As St Andrew's was a collegiate church at that time, the two ministers took turns in leading worship. It appears that the Town Council, having built the church, was not that good at maintaining it. The record shows that before 1843 there were continual problems with keeping the church warm and in good repair. Indeed in 1860, an Act of Parliament was passed transferring the administration and custody of the city churches to the Body of Ecclesiastical Commissioners. The church had fallen into a state of disrepair and discomfort, "… its walls never having been lathed" (and thus plastered). If this is correct it seems quite astonishing that the church, noted for its beautiful interior, had gone for nearly one hundred years without its walls being plastered. Given its location and beauty and the illustrious nature of many of its members, it is easy to understand why in the early years of the nineteenth century St Andrew's was the most influential church in Edinburgh. The General Assemblies of 1841, 1842, and 1843 met in the church, and it would be the location of the Disruption in 1843.

So what was the texture of St Andrew's Church from its beginning in 1784 to 1843? It was very much a professional-class church, made up of lawyers, doctors, bankers and other professional people. No doubt that the idea of gaining a professional network was implicit in some minds when they joined. For example, in 1810 Mr. John Bonnar, House-Painter, was ordained onto the Session. With so many new houses being built and requiring decoration, perhaps Mr. Bonnar spotted a commercial opportunity. On the other hand, with so many of the legal fraternity coming to worship at the church, it would seem foolish for a lawyer or writer not to be seen and known by his colleagues. But this accumulation of leadership in St Andrew's must have implied a loss of it in other places. Leadership in the Old Town was leaking away. Moreover, the practice of renting seats surely posed a problem. With almost all the seats being let to the wealthy and their domestic servants, it would be difficult for the ordinary person coming to worship on a Sunday morning to obtain a seat. The church was very popular with the military and with couples intending to get married. And yet for its class structure it showed considerable concern for the poor, operating a Sunday School, a day school and a chapel.

In the historical records pertaining to St Andrew's it is instructive to note the authors' judgments about the ministers. What qualities are highlighted and appreciated and what are not? On the whole, it is the minister's preaching and academic ability which appears most important. Little is said about pastoral care or organisational ability. A poor preacher, no matter what his other qualities might be, is a disappointment. The following is a quotation referring to Dr Alexander Grant in 1813. It very bluntly expresses the centrality of preaching and throws a light on the relationship between St Andrew's and St George's:

"Dr. Blair's sermons seem to have been the model he has sought to imitate in inculcating religious truth. Being naturally of a phlegmatic temperament he has few or none of the qualities necessary to constitute a popular preacher."[10]

The church was certainly operative in the New Town during the first part of the nineteenth century, but dark clouds were forming. They were comprised of issues over patronage, evangelical zeal, and the pluralities. In 1843 a major event would split the Church of Scotland. It was the Disruption, but it is surprising that in several of the original sources for the history of the church neither the clouds nor the storm that followed are explicitly mentioned.

[10] *Christie, p. 59*

CHAPTER 4

St George's Church 1814-1843

In 1800 Charlotte Square was completed. Edinburgh Town Council had established St Andrew's Church in 1774. Now there was need for another church to meet the worship needs of the people of Edinburgh. According to the Act of Parliament, the Lord Provost, Magistrates and the Council had the right to enter into contracts for the building and completion of another church as soon as the population reached five thousand inhabitants. It must be the case then that by about 1810 the population of the New Town had exceeded five thousand. So the Council agreed to build St George's Church at the other end of George Street. The location originally prescribed for the church by James Craig was still available; whether by design or accident isn't clear. Plans for St George's were drawn up by Robert Reid, in preference to a submission from Robert Adam. The estimated cost was £18,000 and the actual cost £33,194. The foundation stone was laid on May 14, 1811, and the tavern bill for the stone laying amounted to £81!

As St George's, like St Andrew's, was a burgh church, the town council along with the General Presbytery had the authority to appoint the minister. It would be financially convenient if the Council could secure a minister who could fill the pews and thus obtain a good return from the seat-rents.[11] The minister chosen was Dr. Andrew Mitchell Thomson, who had been minister at Sprouston, Perth, and New Greyfriars. He was a good choice, a powerful and popular preacher. Before long, every seat was taken and occupied, once again taking in members from the Old Town. As in the case of St Andrew's, it was the law fraternity that dominated the membership. The first Kirk-Session was made up of the Minister, a Lord, a Banker, a Magistrate, two Advocates, four Writers to the Signet, the Rector of the High School and one other.

In the church throughout Scotland there was a growing division between two parties: the Moderates and the Evangelicals. However, these labels must not be understood in the sense they are used today. The Moderates were just that: reasonable and accommodating but not very enthusiastic. They were happy enough with the way things were, with the existing establishment. David MacGlagan describes the atmosphere, although he believes that it is beginning to give way:

"... the general atmosphere was intensely worldly, cold and indifferent; and church-going, as a rule, was attended to very much because it was generally considered a proper thing to be done."[12]

---

[11] *David MacLagan, A History of St George's Church 1814-1843 and St George's Free Church 1843-1873, p.9*

[12] *MacLagan, p.15*

Andrew Mitchell Thomson was an Evangelical, and his approach, according to MacGlagan, was different. In contrast to this generally cold and indifferent atmosphere, Dr. Thomson's sermons were marvellous. They drew such crowds that it was difficult for the seat-holders to get through the crowds standing at the door and in the corridors to get to their seats. It was at this stage of things that St George's was regarded as the most influential church in Edinburgh, and undoubtedly this was due to the numerous abilities of Andrew Mitchell Thomson himself. He composed music, was interested in education, and founded and edited a journal entitled *Christian Instructor*. He was a leader in the anti-slavery movement. An excerpt from a sermon entitled "Slavery not sanctioned by but condemned by Christianity" provides an example of powerful preaching:

"From this it is clear that Scripture considers slavery as a great and essential evil, and liberty as a great and essential good ..."
"If you introduce the principles and sentiments of Christianity into the heart of any individual, you introduce into his heart the very elements of freedom-you infuse that which he feels to be at eternal variance with any species of bondage-you prepare him for the throwing off the yoke, with an energy which may be calm and secret, but which is also potent and irresistible in its operation."[13]

Perhaps it's not surprising that because of such preaching there was some rivalry between St Andrew's and St George's. Returning to the criticism of Dr. Grant we saw in the last chapter, the commentator went on to say that:

[13] *Andrew Thomson, The Christian Instructor, MD.COC.XXIX, p.371*

"Previous to the opening of St George's Church in 1814, St Andrew's was one of the best filled churches in Edinburgh from its locality; but the powerful and energetic preaching of Dr. Andrew Thomson immediately drew crowds to St George's and attracted many from St Andrew's Church."[14]

But Thomson is also remembered as a caring and good pastor, an aspect of the ministry that is not always mentioned as being important. As was the case with St Andrew's, St George's was given part of St Cuthbert's parish.

As well as slavery, Thomson was concerned about *pluralities* in the church, a practice that went back many centuries. A man could be appointed to several "benefices" or income-producing positions in the church, drawing income from each of them, and yet not giving full service to any. It had been a practice in the Roman Catholic Church and the Church of England, where a priest could be appointed to hold several offices at the same time, meaning that he would necessarily be absent for part of the year. The Reformation in Scotland regarded this practice as one of the corruptions of the church. Yet in Scotland in the eighteenth and nineteenth centuries it was often the practice that the minister of an important church might also hold a professorship in the university. Thus, for example, William Moodie was inducted to St Andrew's in 1787, but he was also appointed to the Chair of Hebrew in Edinburgh University in 1793. He would have drawn an income from both positions. Thomson must have argued that it was impossible to do justice to two important positions at the same time. A few years later, in 1824, The Reverend Robert Burns, minister of St George's in Paisley, would formalise that objection. Burns wrote a book entitled *Pluralities in the*

Church of Scotland: Examined, arguing against what he called "unions of offices" instead of "benefices". Holding two offices, he said, necessarily means the withdrawal of one's attention from one office or the other. He gave as an example a minister in Glasgow, a "... Professor of logic, who holds, at the same time, the pastoral charge of fifteen thousand souls."[15]

More importantly, Thomson was also opposed to the system of patronage, and of this more will be said later. One might well gain the impression that Thomson was, in Benjamin Franklin's words, "disputatious". Indeed, MacGlagan writes that Thomson was sometimes "carried to extremes."[16] While this may well be true, it does appear that he seems to hold the moral high-ground regarding the controversial issues he tackled. His preaching, in the context of the make-up of St George's at that time raises an intriguing question. How difficult was it to proclaim such liberal views in that congregation? Remember the composition of the first Kirk-Session: *a Lord, a Banker, a Magistrate, two Advocates, four Writers to the Signet, the Rector of the High School and one other.* The disposition of any Kirk-session is always in the minister's mind. It would seem unlikely that these elders would be terribly liberal in their outlook, so it must have taken some courage to preach as Thomson did. Looking back many years later, Murdo Ewen Macdonald speaks of the "turbulence" of his first two years in St George's West He writes:

"I introduced a number of changes which the conservative element in the congregation resented and strongly resisted. One of the Judges in the Kirk Session was my toughest opponent. A

[15] Robert Burns, *Pluralities of Offices in the Church of Scotland*, p.10
[16] MacLagan, p.17

powerful orator when defending the status quo, he could become vituperative."[17]

While there was clearly some rivalry between the two churches, there was also some sharing of mission. The church worked with St Andrew's to support and maintain the Sunday School begun in the Assembly Rooms. St George's, now a wealthy church like St Andrew's, was also concerned about the poor and was committed to charitable causes. A collection for foreign missions in 1840 raised the sum or £33 8s. St George's annual collection around 1840, excluding seat-rents, was £6000. It contributed £500 per year to the Charity Workhouse for the Poor, an institution built towards the middle of the eighteenth century at Port Bristo. By 1778, the Workhouse could accommodate 484 adults and 180 children. The church established schools in Rose Street and William Street, and also purchased a building in Young Street for the work of a missionary.

How were the churches of the New Town doing then, after a few years of settling in? Both are "burgh" churches, which meant that they were founded by the town council. Their ministers have been chosen and appointed by the town council and General Presbytery. The institutions are the "patrons". Both churches enjoy very wealthy congregations, having drawn their membership from the professional classes of the Old Town. Their high seat-rents and locations mean that the churches in the New Town had only a handful of poor members between them.[18]

[17] Murdo Ewen Macdonald, Padre Mac: The Man from Harris, p.148
[18] Andrew Drummond and James Bulloch, The Church in Victorian Scotland 1843-1874, p.60

However, from a financial point of view the ministers of the New Town Churches were doing rather well. Edinburgh city ministers in 1835 received a stipend of £548, the highest in Scotland. Most other ministers received stipends round about £150, and the average pay for a working man was £1 per week.[19] But it is very important to maintain a level-headed view when considering the actual worship of the church in this period of time. It would, for example, be quite incorrect to think that worship in the "good old days" was always lively, inspirational and enthusiastically supported. The opposite was true. Drummond and Bulloch write that:

"For two centuries, if judged by the standards of most of Christendom, Scottish worship had been peculiarly defective, colourless, drab, dominated by doctrinal preaching, and lacking in devotion."[20]

Andrew Mitchell Thomson thought that the prayers in most churches were awful. Scripture lessons were not read, men often wore their hats during the service, and worshippers started to leave at the beginning of the benediction. The congregation sat for hymns and prayers. Children were always baptised in private, there was no funeral service at the grave, and weddings consisted only of the exchange of vows and a short prayer. Thomson tried to improve the standard of the music in worship. He composed hymn tunes, including St George's Edinburgh assisted by a member, R.A. Smith from Paisley. Smith had lived in Reading in England and had gained musical experience by being a member of the choir and a bandsman. The ministry of Andrew Mitchell Thomson represents another *turning point* in the story. His very vocal

[19] *Drummond and Bulloch, p.61*
[20] *Drummond and Bulloch, p.201*

opposition to slavery, interest in education and attempts to improve worship were surely significant and influential.

It is true that the New Town churches had all the seats rented out and were packed for worship on Sunday, but what drew people to these churches? Judging from everything we've seen it was clearly the sermon, but largely the oratory rather than the theology. People went to hear the great orator, the man who could speak intelligently and without notes for a long time. The original source material invariably focuses on how good a preacher the minister is, with very little said about his skills as pastor and organiser. Indeed, the emphasis on the sermon meant that it became convenient for the minister to neglect his other responsibilities. It is said that some ministers in the Church of Scotland, although they read widely and vigorously, had little contact with the people in their parishes and did only the essential services such as funerals and weddings. One is said to have come to the church only once a week to dictate his two sermons to his secretary. There might therefore be little connection between the minister and the parish or the community.[21] Preaching has become, in part, *entertainment*. There weren't many other avenues of entertainment on a Sunday, so why not listen to the great preacher? But if the New Town churches were full, that wasn't the case everywhere: "In the Royalty of Edinburgh, the Old Town from the Castle to Holyrood, only 7 out of 27,000 attended an Old Town church, and few could have made their way down to the churches of the wealthy New Town."[22]

[21] *Ian Gilmour, In conversation*
[22] *Drummond and Bulloch, p.36*

Andrew Mitchell Thomson deserves great respect as the first minister of the charge, for his passion, his courage in dealing with controversial social issues and his attempt to improve worship. He died suddenly on the February 9, 1831, on his way home from a meeting of the presbytery. His sudden and early death clearly stunned the congregation. After Thomson's untimely death, St George's called the Reverend James Martin of Stockbridge. However, Mr. Martin was not a well man and died in 1834. St George's then called Robert Smith Candlish, who was inducted in 1834. Mr. Candlish was to play a very important role in the life both of St George's and of the Church of Scotland over the next dozen years, for the dark clouds which had been gathering over the question of patronage were now doing so at an even faster rate.

CHAPTER 5

The Disruption

By 1843 many changes had taken place in Edinburgh. The Mound road had been opened, Charlotte Square had been completed, the head office of the Bank of Scotland had been built, there had been a protest meeting against West Indian slavery, five coaches per day now ran between Edinburgh and Glasgow, the New Town had been completed – making the Old Town a slum – and the Edinburgh to Glasgow railway line was up and running. But in 1843 a far more important event was to occur in the Church of Scotland. Just as the expansion of Edinburgh into the New Town changed everything in the town, so the Disruption changed everything for the church. A major limb of the whole church was rendered into a number of smaller and weaker branches. There is no single cause or simple way to explain the Disruption. There were several different underlying factors and there are several differing interpretations of this event. A full analysis of the disruption is beyond the scope of this little history, so a very limited examination will have to suffice.

There were, as we have indicated, two "religious" parties in the church at the time: the Moderates, and the Popular party or Evangelicals. Conflict between them had been going on for ten years, ever since the General Assembly had passed two acts: *The Chapels Act* and the *Veto Act*. *The Chapels Act* raised many new extension charges or chapels into full status in the established church, giving them parishes and granting their ministers authority in the church courts that they had not previously had. This effectively shifted the balance of power to the Evangelicals, and created resentment among the Moderates.

Up until this time, the system of patronage controlled the appointment of ministers. Only the laird or landowner, the town council, or the head of a corporation could nominate or present the candidate for the vacant charge. We have already seen how the Town Council chose the ministers for the two burgh churches. This was called *patronage*. The issue is a very important one. Would a minister appointed by the laird ever be likely to proclaim a word critical of his practices or views? Would his sympathies on crucial issues lie with the landowner or the people? There was growing opposition to patronage. Should not the people, the members of a church, have the right to appoint the minister? After all, people were now gaining the ability to elect officials to the government. People like Andrew Mitchell Thomson had been calling for the complete abolition of the principle of patronage, although others preferred a more gradual approach. Thomas Chalmers, for example, wanted to retain the system but to insert a popular element into it. Under the terms of the *Veto Act* the patron would present a candidate for the office, and while the presbytery would examine the candidate, the congregation could still veto him. Even if the presbytery had passed the candidate, should a majority of the male members oppose the patron's nominee, the presbytery was duty bound to reject him.

The matter came to a head in 1834 when the patron of the parish of Auchterarder presented Robert Young to fill the vacancy. After hearing Mr. Young preach twice, a large majority of the congregation – 287 male heads of families out of 330 – voted against him. The presbytery accordingly rejected the candidate. However, the matter was appealed to the Court of Session, who upheld the appeal and ordered the presbytery to admit Mr. Young. Several weeks later the General Assembly took up the matter and appealed to the House of Lords. A year later the law lords ruled against, declaring that the patron's rights were absolute and that no objections by parishioners were relevant. The tension increased when several cases similar to the Auchterarder case followed. Thomas Chalmers and others then turned to Parliament to try and find a solution. The solution wasn't coming. The House of Commons rejected the call for a special Parliamentary inquiry into the state of affairs in Scotland. The General Assembly of 1842 expressed their support for the total abolition of Patronage. But in January of 1843 the Government gave its final refusal to repeal the Patronage Act. Now the stage was set for the drama.

The General Assembly of 1843 met in St Andrew's Church. The Moderator, David Welsh, did not follow the usual routine. *"Instead of making up the roll of members and installing his successor, he read out a lengthy Protest against the conditions imposed on the Church by the State—conditions which made it impossible for him and his associates to accept the privileges of*

Establishment any longer. He then left the chair and the building, followed by some two hundred ministers and elders who shared his views. Through an excited crowd, and joined by many sympathisers, they processed to the Tanfield Hall in Canonmills, where they constituted themselves 'The Church of Scotland-Free', and signed a Deed of Demission renouncing the many benefits of Establishment."[23]

By the following Tuesday 450 ministers across the country had signed the Deed of Demission. In doing so they had given up their positions, their manses, their glebes and their stipends, amounting to annual revenue of £100,000. It was an unparalleled act of determination and courage. This would set the course of history for the next eighty-six years. Within five years the Free Church had erected more than seven hundred churches, more than five hundred schools and had also built New College.

But was it necessary? There is argument about whether the final drama and conclusion was what had really been intended. Some think that the Evangelicals did not really wish to break with the established church but only with the state. They had assumed they would control the General Assembly of 1843 and so could break with the state rather than the whole church. By leaving positions and stipends and the rest they would do so as the church and not merely as a party. In fact, the argument goes, they misjudged the level of support from those in the middle and did not have the majority. On the other hand, the Evangelicals had certainly prepared the way to disruption by making ready an organisation and alternative places of worship. In any event, the deed was done, and one great branch, the Scottish branch, of the Church of Jesus

---

[23] A.C. Cheyne, *The Ten Years' Conflict and the Disruption*, p. 11

Christ had been rent. There would over time be several other splits. The Free Church had many talented and courageous ministers, and it also possessed an enormous drive to succeed. It would undoubtedly do well. But the established church would survive as well. The trouble was that in most parishes there would now be two of everything-church buildings, congregations, ministers and manses! This amounted to an enormous waste of resources. Sometimes families and friends would be split as well, and such disputes could be bitter and long-lasting.

Moreover, another unanticipated consequence arose in some places. The Free Church had carried out ambitious plans for the building of churches. These were sometimes supported by wealthy individuals who were not necessarily members of the church. When they loaned money for such projects they might well look for a revenue return through seat-rents.[24] And where the wealthy donor was a member of the church he might well expect to wield power in the life of the congregation. Having done away with patronage, it sometimes simply returned wearing a different face. The Disruption in Scotland amounted to a major event in the growth of the tree, and St Andrew's and St George's were at the very centre of this event. It was initiated in St Andrew's, and the eventual leader of the Free Church would be Robert Candlish of St George's.

[24] *Drummond and Bulloch, p.48*

CHAPTER 6

Branches

The Disruption fundamentally changed the nature of the church tree. Limbs became branches and branches sprouted more branches. A detailed account of this sprouting is beyond our scope in this book. The best account, with a diagram indicating the effects in Edinburgh, is to be found in Ian Dunlop's book.[25] A much simplified version follows.

The Reverend John Bruce, the minister of St Andrew's at the Disruption, had walked down the road to Canonmills with one elder and 200-300 members to form Free St Andrew's. This congregation then worshipped in a building built on the back green of 80 George Street. The Reverend Thomas Clark, married to the daughter of the first minister William Greenfield, became the next minister of St Andrew's. He was followed at the original St Andrew's by Thomas Crawford, John Stuart, Arthur Gordon, Peter Hunter, George Christie, William Blackburn, and James Stuart Thomson in 1941. Two free churches, St Luke's Free and Tolbooth Free, united in 1891 to form Queen Street Free. But efforts were being made

[25] *Dunlop, The Kirks of Edinburgh*

to unite the two denominations, and so in 1929 the Church of Scotland and the United Free Church were united, and the first General Assembly of the united church was gathered in St Andrew's church. The drama surrounding the Disruption was apparently not repeated at the Reunion of the two churches. It is difficult to find much evidence about the nature of the coming together of the churches, but it did happen. Limbs were slowly being bound together. A lesser union was created when in 1947 the original St Andrew's united with Queen Street. In 1948 Donald Davidson was called to St Andrew's, having served as the minister of South Leith. Davidson had a fine academic background and was a gifted preacher, producing a number of works containing sermons and addresses. He died in 1970. The Davidsons' son Kemp was a noted advocate and judge and also served as Procurator for the Church of Scotland.

Meanwhile, at the other end of George Street, the Reverend Robert Smith Candlish, along with eight elders and a number of members walked away from St George's and moved into what was known as "The Brick Church" in Castle Terrace. It is interesting that the money had been raised for this building in preparation for the Disruption, a fact which sheds light on the thinking and organisation of Dr. Candlish and other leaders. This church was known as St George's Free. Shortly thereafter a site was purchased on Lothian Road. The church built on this site opened in 1845, with twenty-one elders, twenty deacons and one thousand members.[26] Only twenty years later the Caledonia Railway wished to buy the site to construct a new station. A site was located on Shandwick

---

[26] Dunlop, p. 159. The names "St George's Free" and "Free St George's" are both used in the literature

Place, and in 1867 the Earl of Dalhousie laid the foundation stone for a new church. Designed by David Bryce, the oblong building had galleries on three sides. This church opened in 1869, with Dr. Candlish preaching in the morning and Oswald Dykes in the afternoon. A report of the opening service in 1869 indicated that "following the prevailing fashion, a pulpit has been dispensed with, and instead a tasteful platform has been erected in the apse at the north end of the building." It is a curious statement, for the tasteful platform is spacious enough upon which to walk around, and it certainly functions as a pulpit. St George's Free became St George's UF in 1900 and then St George's West in 1929.[27]

Candlish was born in Edinburgh, but his early life was spent in Glasgow. After serving several assistantships, he came through to be minister of St George's West. Along with Thomas Chalmers, Candlish was highly influential in bringing about the Disruption. His strong leadership, first in the Disruption and then as minister of St George's West, was very important, for it set a pattern for many who followed. In this sense it represents a turning point in our story, or at least a *learning point*. It's worthwhile spending some time examining his theology.

Since Candlish took much responsibility for establishing the new Free Church, it is instructive to ask him a key question: what exactly is the church? An insight into an answer to this question may be found in his commentary on Romans in the section entitled "The Christian in his relation to God" under the title "Consecration to God."

[27] Dunlop, pp. 159-160

"*Now it is as thus knowing God, who is a spirit; knowing thus, also, ourselves as spiritual men; and knowing, above all, the foot on which we stand with our God and Father; – that we are called, as priests, to present a sacrifice of praise. May we not decide and determine for ourselves, according to these considerations, what sort of sacrifice is suitable and appropriate? What is worthy of God? What is worthy of ourselves? What sort of sacrifice may God be expected to accept? What sort of sacrifice, in the full view of all the circumstances, may be regarded as our 'reasonable service?' At all events, tried by such a test, how miserably will many a sacrifice and service that we are apt to present to fail and be found wanting! Form, ceremony, routine; heartless prayers, however long; ostentatious alms, however large; bodily exercise, whether in the way of easy compliance with outward rites, or in the way of painful inward self-mortification; enforced obedience; reluctant abstinence from pleasure; the cold and cheerless performance of duty; all or any of these kinds of worship – all similar methods of serving God – we can bring to this criterion. Is it such a sacrifice of praise and thanksgiving that a reconciled God and Father should in fairness be asked to accept? Is it such a sacrifice of praise and thanksgiving that we, his reconciled children, may be reasonably asked to offer? Is it such a sacrifice of praise and thanksgiving that should signalise and seal so thorough a repairing of the breach caused by sin between our God and us, as that which the High Priest's sacrifice of atonement effects? Surely, if it is felt by the universal moral instinct of all men to be true, that the blood of bulls and goats cannot take away sin – it must, be felt also by the universal spiritual instinct, of all those whose sins are taken away, by the blood of a better ransom, to be not less true, that formal worship, or obedience rendered in the spirit of bondage, is not the sacrifice which a redeeming God can worthily accept, and is not a 'reasonable service' on the part of the people whom he redeems.*"[28]

[28] Robert Smith Candlish, "The Christian in Relation to God", www.newble.co.uk, pp.4-5

We are as priests, Candlish argues, to present to God a sacrifice of praise. What is a sufficient sacrifice? Not form or ceremony or routine, not heartless prayers, not ostentatious alms, not abstinence from pleasure or the cold and cheerless performance of duty. Candlish thus largely dismisses all the things that happen in worship, even though this is central to the life of the church. Formal worship, at least not the worship that is rendered in the spirit of bondage, is not acceptable to God. So it is fair to ask, if we are all called to be priests, what we are to do?

"I beseech you therefore brethren, that ye present yourselves a sacrifice. And let it be yourselves in Christ; let it be Christ in you. For thus only can it be a sacrifice "living and holy." When Christ presents himself a sacrifice of atonement, be you one with him in his doing so. When you present yourselves a sacrifice of praise, let him be one with you in your doing so. Let the two presentations be ever going on together, simultaneously, unitedly. The presentation by Christ of himself as the sacrifice of atonement is always going on in the sanctuary above. There, in the true holy place, he is always ministering as your great High Priest, having his own blood to offer, ever freshly flowing, and freshly efficacious to cleanse from all sin ... In a corresponding manner, let your presentation of yourselves, as a sacrifice of thanksgiving be always going on in the sanctuary here below; the only sanctuary now owned on earth – the deep and sacred shrine of a believing heart ... There is the sin-offering of the living and holy body of Christ once for all, and there is the thank-offering of the living and holy Church, which is his 'mystical' body, the fullness of him who filleth all in all." (Eph. 1.23)[29]

[29] *Candlish, pp.7-8*

We are to present ourselves to Christ *in our hearts*. The real sanctuary here on earth is the *heart*. The actual sanctuary of the church or congregation, with its formal worship and its community, is of lesser importance. It appears to be important only insofar as it provides a place for people to gather and hear the preacher. The real body of Christ is not the tangible community of believers, but a mystical body. It's hard to imagine Candlish taking an interest in building up the community, in the dynamics of life together. What matters is a place to preach the gospel rather than the lives who those who hear and respond. What is striking, at least in this section of his commentary, is that Candlish does not deal with the very next part of the letter to the Romans, where Paul speaks about a real body with many members, and all the members having various gifts. It would seem that the gifts of prophecy, ministry, teaching, exhortation, generosity in giving, and compassion and cheerfulness have little value for Candlish. This is not a theology for the community, but for the individual, with transactions taking place *in the heart*. This theology of unilateral proclamation establishes or at least continues a pattern which will prevail for years to come. Indeed, it is still the case that in many, if not most, of our theological colleges very little instruction is provided on the sociology of the congregation as a living community. The leadership skills required to enable people to lead, or moderate a Kirk Session or board, or deal with finance are seldom discussed. The result is that many ministers are ill-equipped to exercise leadership in a congregation of real men and women. James Gustafson, in dealing with the church as a moral decision-maker writes the following:

"The congregation is a place of speaking and hearing: often this has meant the minister speaking and the people hearing, or the

Word of God is the speech and men are the auditors ... Rather than rely upon open discourse and run the risks that are involved in it, most ministers and church leaders select other available options. A common one is reliance upon the persuasive power of personality to bring support to some moral judgment or cause that the minister in his isolation has decided is worthy of loyalty and action. Ministers often are very unwilling to enter discourse; they prefer to come to conclusions without its benefit, and then often seek in pulpit or in one-to-one relations to bring men to their own point of view.[30]

Candlish's dismissal of the church as a genuine community in favour of a "sanctuary in the heart", along with his view of preaching as the central event of worship, does not represent so much a turning-point as a reflection of a pre-existing pattern. But they do reinforce such a pattern and reinforce it particularly in the Free Church. A powerful and great preacher can function as a great oratorical entertainer, but what happens when other more attractive forms of entertainment emerge?

James Oswald Dykes was called to provide assistance to Dr. Candlish, which he did from 1861 until 1864. Following Dykes, Alexander Whyte was called to assist Dr. Candlish at St George's Free. By all accounts, Whyte was a very remarkable man. He was born out of wedlock to Janet Thomson in Kirriemuir. Janet did not marry his father, John Whyte, who departed for the United States. As a boy Alexander went to church three times on a Sunday. Whyte's mother lacked the money to fund his elementary education, so at age ten he gave it up to work as a herd-boy. At thirteen he became an

---

[30] James Gustafson, *The Church as Moral Decision-Maker*, pp. 90-91

apprentice shoemaker, and it is said that he employed a young boy to hold up a book for him to read while making shoes. At the age of eighteen he became a schoolmaster at the single-room school in Padanaram.[31] He took up a position at the Free Church School in Airlie, where the minister taught him Latin and Greek. Desperate for more education but still lacking the funds, Whyte wrote to his father in the United States, requesting financial help. Whyte's father was apparently a successful businessman. Perhaps surprisingly, financial support was granted, and he enrolled at King's College, where the library became a haunt. In 1862 he graduated and entered New College, Edinburgh, where he studied under Dr. Candlish, among others. He finished New College in 1866, was licensed, and went to be an assistant at Free St John's in Glasgow. In 1870 he came to assist Dr. Candlish at Free St George's, remaining there for almost fifty years. In 1909 he succeeded Dr. Marcus Dods as principal of New College.

Whyte was a powerful preacher and teacher, appealing to the conscience and making real the reality of sin. Perhaps due to his abundant reading, he had a special way with words. He could, it is reported, paint vivid word pictures. Moreover, perhaps because of his experience of poverty, his preaching was down to earth and appealed to the common man. The oft-quoted phrase regarding Whyte is that he was: "Always like fire on a cold day." Here is an excerpt from one of Whyte's sermons under the rubric "Lord, teach us to pray." His text is Luke 11:5-8.

"It is night. It is midnight. The night is dark. The lights are out and everybody is in bed. 'Friend! Lend me three loaves! For a

---

[31] *An excellent summary of Alexander Whyte's life may be found in an article by Maureen Bradley, "Alexander Whyte – His Life and Sermons", 1997*

friend of mine in his journey is come to me, and I have nothing to set before him!' He knocks again. 'Friend, lend me three loaves!' He waits awhile and then he knocks again. 'Friend, friend, I must have three loaves!' 'Trouble me not: the door is now shut; I cannot rise and give thee!' He is dumb, for a time. He stands still. He turns to go home. But he cannot go home. He dare not go home. He comes back. He knocks again. 'Friend!' he cries, till the dogs bark at him. He puts his ear to the door. There is a sound inside, and the light of a candle shines through the hole of the door. The bars of the door are drawn back, and he gets not three loaves only but as many as he needs. 'And I say unto you, Ask, and it shall be given you; seek and you shall find; knock and it shall be opened unto you.'"[32]

Whyte's ability to speak in simple and picture language (It's dark; the lights are out; he cannot go home; the dogs bark; an ear to the door; a sound inside, a light though the crack) would capture and hold the listener's attention immediately. This is great preaching, and it is interesting to compare and contrast it with Robert Candlish's. But Whyte was also a great teacher and he instituted classes for young people on many different subjects. Among all the ministries considered in this book, Alexander Whyte's work must be seen as a high and signal achievement.

In 1896 Hugh Black came as assistant. Black was also a forceful preacher, his sermons being "original, brilliant and suggestive". The two men seemed to perform well together, and generated several clichés. It was said that "Dr. Whyte blackballed sinners in the morning and Dr. Black whitewashed them in the evening"[33]. The *Glasgow Herald* commented that:

[32] www.oChristian.com, *Lord, Teach us to Pray* 14
[33] *The Glasgow Herald*, April 8, 1953

"Whyte and Black as an ecclesiastical firm may have occasioned mild jests and glowing anecdotes, but they were incomparable as a pair, and a visit to Edinburgh was not reckoned complete without at least one service in Free St George's."

Hugh Black became famous, and he was invited to give lectures at Union Theological Seminary in New York in 1906. Following his lectures he was invited to become the professor of Practical Theology at Union. Reporting on one of his sermons at Fifth Avenue Presbyterian Church, the *New York Times* commented in its headline that Mr. Black believes that a "nation's strength lies in its moral rather than its material development." The article went on to report, curiously, that Mr. Black "reads his sermons."[34]

Here is an extract from that same sermon. The text was Isaiah 13: 12:

"Our Christian civilization has no place in it for some of the wrongs of men and women common in the pagan world. We have for one thing been taught at least something of the sacredness of human life. There is a public conscience which would prevent some of the hideous evils of ancient Babylon and Rome. Our Government and commerce have been Christianized to a very large extent. But the Babylonian spirit has not left the world, and every great civilization is menaced by the temptation of forgetfulness of God, cruelty of sheer force, insolence of pride, and the empty trust of wealth. Our foes are the old foes with a new face. Every empire is dogged by the same temptation – to rely wholly upon material strength, and to add arrogance of mind to luxury of life."

---

[34] *The New York Times, September 2, 1901*

"Not once nor twice have the resources of civilization proved helpless when the morale of a people has crumbled down. Nor once nor twice in history has it been seen that the last line of defence has been not material, but moral. Not once nor twice has the world witnessed the strongest nations rotting to their doom, when the moral laws of life were disregarded, when the purity of the family, the purity of justice, was tarnished when wealth accumulated, and self-indulgence became the ideal."[35]

Clearly, Hugh Black made quite a lasting impact in the United States. A September 2010 advertisement indicates that Mary Baker Eddy, of Christian Science fame appreciated Hugh Black's book entitled *Friendship*.

Dr. Candlish had refused to countenance having an organ in the church. However, Hugh Black persuaded the Kirk Session to install an instrument. He then, apparently, travelled to Nottingham to hear Alfred Hollins, a blind organist, play. Upon the first hearing, Hollins was offered the position as church organist and remained at St George's Free for the rest of his life. Alfred Hollins made many tours giving organ recitals, including Australia and New Zealand, South Africa, Germany, and the United States. It is estimated that he travelled some 600,000 miles on his tours.[36] Alfred Hollins also composed music for the organ, in all at least thirty-six pieces, including "Triumphal March" and "Rejoice in the Lord."

Hollins made some instructive comments about the ministers with whom he worked regarding their attitudes towards music and their choice of praise for worship. He writes that

[35] *The New York Times, September 2, 1901*
[36] *"Alfred Hollins", Wikipedia*

Alexander Whyte took meticulous care in choosing the praise, and the praise list always got to the organist by Friday. Hugh Black left the selection of all the praise to the organist, except for the last hymn, but he also wanted to have the praise list by the previous Sunday. He would then weave portions of one or more hymns into the prayers. John Kelman introduced "sheet" anthems, which Hollins considered to be of real benefit. Kelman chose all the praise himself, but Hollins considered that his method of doing so left out too many hymns. James Black, according to Hollins, left the selection of the praise to the organist, although he had favourites which he liked to insert. He was, however, reluctant to use unfamiliar hymns.[37]

The issue of music in worship, and particularly the use of hymns in worship, is relevant. It is undoubtedly the case that a congregation learns most of its theology from the hymns that it repeatedly sings over the years, and yet this too is a subject rarely dealt with in theological college. For many ministers the choice of hymns is rather an afterthought, and it has been known for a minister not to choose the praise until just prior to the service of worship on Sunday. So there are important questions to ask and answer: who chooses the praise, the minister or the musician? On what basis is it chosen: with an eye on the words of the sermon or an eye on the music? Is the praise boring or tedious because too many hymns are in the same key or employ a similar four-line stanza? If new hymns are used, how are they introduced to the congregation? Is gender or old-fashioned language in hymns a problem, and should hymns be altered to deal with the problem? Indeed, is gender language in theology a problem for believers?

[37] Alfred Hollins, *The Tradition of St George's West*, pp. 80-82

James Kelman was called as colleague and successor to Alexander Whyte in 1907. He also was a fine preacher, leaving in 1919 to be the minister of Fifth Avenue Presbyterian Church in New York. Kelman was followed in 1921 by Hugh Black's brother, James Macdougall Black. James Black was also a fine preacher, and the queues of people coming for the evening service continued, some of whom would need to sit on the pulpit or gallery steps. James Black published several books on preaching and delivered lectures on the subject in Virginia, Melbourne and Edinburgh. In 1931 He was asked if he would receive a call from Marble Collegiate Church in New York City. He clearly decided not to do so and remained as minister until 1948. James Black served as chaplain to George VI and was highly respected by the congregation. In 1931 he produced a short history of the congregation.

Edinburgh was still regarded as a centre of excellence in several disciplines, especially medicine and science. In this respect mention must be made of several laymen who were notable members in these churches. Joseph Bell was a lecturer in the medical faculty of the University of Edinburgh and a member of St George's West. He was particularly interested in showing the importance of close observation in making a diagnosis and thus became known as a pioneer in forensic science. After 1877 Arthur Conan Doyle served as Bell's clerk at the Royal Infirmary and in the methods of Bell found his inspiration to write his fictional accounts of the great detective Sherlock Holmes. An interesting account of Joseph Bell is given by Julian Barnes in his book *Arthur & George.*[38]

---

[38] *Julian Barnes, Arthur & George, London: Jonathon Cape, p.38*

Over to St Andrew's Church, where a young man attended church almost every Sunday. He had been baptized by Dr. David Ritchie on July 29, 1831. His name was James Clerk Maxwell, and he was to become one of the world's greatest scientists. A humble and self-effacing man, it is clear that even today many Scots have never heard of Maxwell. He went to Edinburgh Academy and at age 13 won the mathematical medal and the first prize for both English and poetry. He attended Edinburgh and Cambridge, and became professor of physics at Marischal College in Aberdeen. Then it was off to King's College London and then Cambridge. His main achievement was "formulating classical electromagnetic theory. This united all previously unrelated observations, experiments, and equations of electricity, magnetism, and optics into a consistent theory."[39] Many scientists consider Maxwell to be the third greatest scientist in history, and Einstein had his picture on the wall beside those of Newton and Faraday. Maxwell also became an elder of the Church of Scotland.

Joseph Houldsworth Oldham (1874-1969) was the Assistant Minister and an elder at St George's Free until he moved to England in 1921. Oldham became the organising secretary of the World Missionary Conference, held in Edinburgh in 1910. Twelve hundred representatives arrived in Edinburgh to set out eight commissions on missions to the modern world. This was a Protestant conference only, and it was driven by the theme "The Evangelization of the World in this Generation." Oldham went on to become the Honorary President of the World Council of Churches. In 2010 the one-hundredth anniversary of the World Missionary Conference was held, once again in Edinburgh.

[39] *"James Clerk Maxwell", Wikipedia*

Back at St George's West, Murdo Ewen Macdonald was called in 1949. A charismatic minister from the island of Harris who had served in the parachute unit during the war, Macdonald was captured by the Germans in North Africa. He spent two years in the Stalag Luft III prison camp in Germany and served as the padre to American troops in the camp, becoming a well-known and much respected figure. He had been the welterweight boxing champion at St Andrews University and had several confrontations with difficult British officers already under his belt. He had been awarded the Bronze Star for outstanding service as chaplain to American prisoners of war. To put it crudely, he was not a man to be messed with.

Macdonald had been the minister in Old Partick in Glasgow before coming to St George's West. Old Partick was, he recalls, a mixed congregation in a parish close to both Glasgow University and to the shipyards on the Clyde. But his move to the west end of Edinburgh was not viewed favourably by everyone. Macdonald recalls the letter he received from George MacLeod:

"Dear Murdo Ewen, I am deeply disappointed. You had a marvellous Church in Glasgow. You were a part-time chaplain in a shipyard within your parish and chaplain to a hospital, also within your parish. You have turned your back on it all and accepted a call from St George's West which is a glorified preaching centre with no social conscience, no more than a middle class religious drawing room."[40]

According to Macdonald, Lord MacLeod later sent a letter apologising for his rudeness and wishing him blessings on his new ministry.

But there was still turbulence in the church. Macdonald wanted to introduce some changes which were vigorously

[40] *Murdo Ewen Macdonald, Padre Mac, p.146*

opposed by a strong Kirk Session. He changed the format of the communion service and a number of members were unhappy. He had to insist that the minister alone was responsible for the conduct of worship. Seat-rents were still in operation at St George's West. This meant that during James Black's ministry queues of people who were not seat-holders would wait for admission to the evening service. To alleviate this problem Macdonald wanted to abolish seat-rents and replace them by the freewill offering envelopes. This too was vigorously opposed, but eventually the minister won the battle.

It's clear that Murdo Ewen Macdonald was perceptive about the changing times and the changing ministry of the church. He introduced a weekly lunch for poorer old age pensioners, a weekly cultural lecture by some prominent speaker: scientists, novelists, poets and editors. Another experiment launched at St George's West was *Cephas,* a club for young people who weren't church members. It met in the crypt of the church and provided entertainment for the members. Macdonald was an enthusiastic supporter of *Cephas* and helped to persuade the Kirk Session to offer the required space, He was also honest and clear-sighted about preaching. He thought that the ideal of preaching one or two great sermons every Sunday was absurd—an impossible ideal.[41] Perhaps only one in three or four sermons might be called great.

As the "Premier Pulpit" in Scotland, St George's West was in an ideal situation to raise money for worthy causes. Earlier, in Alexander Whyte's time, Free St George's paid the stipends of thirty other ministers. Over the following years great amounts

[41] *Macdonald, p.135*

74

of money were contributed to foreign missions. Church extension also benefitted. Seven churches in Edinburgh were founded through the support of this congregation. For example, the church raised £30,000 to support the creation of a new church in the east end of the city, St Martin's.

Murdo Ewen Macdonald's ministry at St George's West was a significant *turning point* in the life of the New Town Churches. For he was a fine preacher and appreciated the value of preaching; he also recognised the need for the church to change in relation to the changing world. One of Macdonald's sentences beautifully sums up the key issue. He asks what the number one threat to the survival of the human race is. He rejects the idea of destruction by nuclear weapons. The greatest threat he argues is "Proximity without community."[42] This recognition is a *turning point*, and we shall return to it.

Back at the original St George's, only about one-third of the congregation had accompanied Dr. Candlish when he walked out of St George's in 1843, so the original church continued under the ministry of the Reverend Robert Horne Stevenson. Stevenson was followed by Archibald Scott and then by Gavin Pagan, who was killed in action in 1917. Charles Taylor succeeded Pagan and remained at St George's for almost thirty-three years. A good organiser and much-loved pastor, his interest was in youth work and he also developed the music of the church. He was followed by James Robert Thomson and then William Cecil Bigwood. However, around 1959 trouble developed in the dome of the building, and it then became apparent that there was dry rot in the structure. The congregation entered into negotiation with St Andrew's

[42] *Macdonald, p.192*

with a view towards union. In 1962 the original St George's and original St Andrew's were linked, and then united in 1964 under Cecil Bigwood. Two original branches had become one.

CHAPTER 7

Life in a Changing Society

The sixties and seventies brought many changes both locally and internationally. In 1956 the tram ran for the last time, and by 1959 the population of the Old Town had declined to 2000 people. In 1969 the Royal Bank of Scotland took over the National Commercial Bank, and the Bank of Scotland absorbed the British Linen Bank. Local government in Scotland was reorganised in 1975. But tumult was even more ominous in the wider world. If the Disruption had created turbulence for the church, then the sixties and seventies brought a more widespread and insidious kind of disturbance. The social order was facing threats on several different fronts and was changing rapidly. There was a Cold War between east and west and a delicate balance of nuclear terror. Racial equality was being demanded and a divisive war was being waged in Vietnam. For the first time, people were seeing the horrors of war on their television screens. The secular city was on the rise, the church was in decline, and some theologians spoke of the "Death of God". Preaching as "entertainment" or "theatre" now had to compete with the entertainment that came into the home on TV. People were no longer equipped to recognise and appreciate literary allusions or even to give full attention to long sermons. The days of full churches and the "Knights of the Pulpit" were numbered. The pattern of worship set long ago by Candlish, Alexander Whyte and the Blacks was perhaps no longer the appropriate pattern. This, however, was not obvious to everyone. With such a long tradition of powerful preachers to draw people to church it was natural for congregations to wish for such preachers. When vacancy committees went out looking for the new minister it was the sermon that took the highest priority. Candidates were compared on the basis of their preaching. If the church was to survive it would need to alter the pattern. Worship would need to call for more than simply a readiness to listen.

At St George's West, the congregation was beginning to recognise and respond to the changing society. Murdo Ewen Macdonald was succeeded by William David Ranald Cattanach. Cattanach was a good preacher as well, but preaching appeared no longer to be so effective in a time of rapid decline for the church in general. He made good use of television as a medium and also played a key role in the development of the Council of West End Churches. Cattanach and his wife Lorna started a church centre and café for office and shop workers at St George's West. It was reported that over a hundred people had volunteered to help in the centre.

Robert Glover succeeded Cattanach. He perceived the dichotomy between the tradition of great preaching and the changing nature of the church and parish, but it proved hard to convert that perception into a new pattern. The existing café was developed, with a minister always present to speak to people. An evening each week was set aside to welcome and feed the homeless. The ideas of "The Open Church" and "In the Witness Box" were pursued.

In 1998 Peter Macdonald became the minister. The building, he believed, was a gift which ought to be available for the community, and particularly for the arts in Edinburgh. The church became a Festival Fringe venue, and the café became the centre of an initiative giving work experience to volunteers with learning difficulties. The Creative Space programme provided an opportunity to engage in spiritual matters with people who were not conventional church-goers.

In 1972 it appears that St Andrew's and St George's was also ready for such a change. The church called William Andrew Wylie to be its minister. Wylie had served in the navy, and while based at Malta, had become friends with Geoff Shaw, who was also attending St Andrew's Kirk. Andrew Wylie's ministry needs to be seen in relation to this friendship with Shaw. After completing his service in the navy, Wylie returned to his native Glasgow, while Shaw entered university in Edinburgh. In 1948 Shaw invited his friend through to Edinburgh to attend a lecture given by John Macmurray, professor of moral philosophy. Shaw was excited by Macmurray's interest in the work of the Jewish philosopher Martin Buber, who distinguished between *I-Thou* relationships and *I-It* relationships. *Thou*, my neighbour, Buber said, is a person and ought never be treated as an *It*, an object in the world. God is the *Eternal Thou*. On the surface, Buber's philosophy is rather straightforward and easy to grasp. We ought to treat people as neighbours rather than as objects to be manipulated for our own purposes. But the fact that it was creating a stir and great interest must point to a society in which mutual concern and care was missing.

Shaw went on to study at New College, at the end of which he won a fellowship to study at Union Theological Seminary in New York. His time at Union was groundbreaking, for while there he became involved in the East Harlem Protestant Ministry. The East Harlem Ministry had been set up by George W. Webber and others to minister in one of the most deprived section of the city, marked by poverty, drugs and crime. Webber's book arose out of that ministry: *God's Colony in Man's World*, which was itself heavily influenced by George MacLeod and the Iona Community. He argued that new wineskins were required for a new and hostile environment. Webber wrote:

"In our modern world of rapid change it is not surprising that our human institutions have fallen behind the pace of modern life. Our churches are still functioning with nineteenth century patterns in the middle of the twentieth century. The assumptions we make about life no longer have much relationship to the facts of our time."[43]

Shaw's East Harlem Protestant Ministry involvement would shape the rest of his life. At the same time he was also influenced by the young German theologian who had been at Union and had gone home to be imprisoned and then hanged by the Third Reich, Dietrich Bonhoeffer. Bonhoeffer would write: *When Christ calls a man he bids him come and die.*

---

[43] George W. Webber, *God's Colony in Man's World*, p.27

There is no doubt that through their close friendship and conversations about Buber, Webber and Bonhoeffer, Geoff Shaw exerted a profound influence on Andrew Wylie. Wylie had gone on to serve as the minister of Whitehill Church in Stepps and then spent six years at the Scots Kirk in Lausanne. From there he went on to be the general secretary of the Scottish Churches Council. This work must have provided him with useful insights about the church as a wider institution. He was not completely at ease with the Church of Scotland as an institution, comparing it with a swimming pool. "It's fine if you can swim and its temperature is OK, but singularly uninviting if you can't."[44] Wylie was clearly good at relating to those outside of the institutional church. He wrote:

"I realised that to talk about secular man could be more of a criticism of the person making the comment than anything else. Because men and women do not have an interest in the institutional church does not justify the implication that they are uninterested in things of the spirit."[45]

When Wylie began his ministry at St Andrew's and St George's, he realised that radical changes were required. The church was at a low point both spiritually and financially. The parish had changed. Tourists and shoppers now walked along the stately streets, and few members now lived in the area. Shops and offices dominated George Street. The traditional pattern of ministry exercised by a parish church appeared to be out of sync with this new environment. The wider world had changed even more radically, and these facts demanded a new kind of vision. Wylie formed plans to build a workplace chaplaincy which could minister to people in the shops and

[44] *Quoted by Johnston McKay in Andrew Wylie's Obituary, The Herald, July 5, 2011*
[45] *McKay, The Herald, July 5, 2011*

offices. The Reverend Robert Mathers would be the first chaplain to shops and offices. St Andrew's and St George's had no hall, so the area under the church was excavated to form the "Undercroft." This provided a comfortable space for lunches and conversation. Wylie decided that worship, using a liturgy suited to lay people, would be held every weekday, with frequent services of communion. All this was radically new. No other church in Scotland had such a ministry. Wylie often stood out on the street to greet passers-by, establishing an image of the church which goes out actively to meet and welcome people instead of waiting passively for them to come in. In a telling phrase, it is said that Andrew Wylie "wore the traditional ministerial gowns but inhabited them in a new way". Wylie's ministry signalled a recovery of the idea of community. This new ministry could provide an antidote to Murdo Ewen Macdonald's concern that the greatest threat to life was "proximity without community." By encouraging a much broader vision of ministry, Wylie released some of the pressure under the demand for the great preacher. This emerging understanding of ministry at St Andrew's and St George's has to be underlined, along with Andrew Wylie's courage in bringing it about. But clearly, there were those in the congregation who supported and made possible such a daring adventure. David Miller and Kemp Davidson were important figures in this respect. Wylie's new kind of ministry represents another *turning point* in the life of the church.

At the same time, other significant things were happening in St Andrew's and St George's. One such development was the beginning of the Christian Aid Book Sale. Started in 1973, and carried out every year since, the sale of books and other items has now raised nearly £2,000,000 for the work of

Christian Aid. Mary Davidson, Cathie Donaldson and others were largely responsible for the creation of this now huge enterprise. The sale receives widespread help and support from both individuals and organisations in the community and has expanded far beyond the sale of books. Mary Levison was also the first woman to be licensed in the Church of Scotland and she was successful in a campaign to permit women to be ordained in the church. In 1978 she served as Associate Minister in St Andrew's and St George's. Several lay members have been at the forefront of developing a more feminist theology. So in a number of different issues the church was showing the way to new ministry.

Andrew Wylie went on to take up a post as chaplain to the North Sea Oil industry and died in 2011. Andrew R.C. McLellan was called in 1986 and continued the idea of the new ministry, serving until 2002.[46] He pursued the goal of variety in worship, with a communion service, all-age service, and traditional form of service every Sunday. Conscious of the many visitors to Edinburgh and the New Town, worship was available every day. Use of the Undercroft was increased, with lunches available daily. This enhanced the ministry of members, with about eighty volunteering to help, not only in preparing and serving food but in conversation. McLellan also served as convener of the Church of Scotland's Church and Nation Committee and as Moderator of the General Assembly. He went on to serve as Her Majesty's Chief Inspector of Prisons for Scotland. He was followed by Roderick Campbell in 2003. Campbell instigated the restoration of the peal, the *Compleat Chymes*, first installed as we have seen in

[46] *It's best to let Andrew McLellan speak for himself here. See his Recollections of a Ministry in Two Churches later in this book*

1798. Mr. Campbell moved on to Lismore, Appin, and Port Appin in 2008. St Andrew's and St George's was united with St George's West in 2010, now to be called *St Andrew's and St George's West*. Ian Y. Gilmour, with valuable parish experience in both Drylaw and South Leith, and a leader of the *Church without Walls* initiative, was called and inducted in 2011. If anyone was suited to continue and expand this new kind of ministry it was Gilmour. Reverend Tony Bryer returned to serve as a workplace chaplain, making contacts and ministering in offices and shops.

CHAPTER 8

Final Observations

Let's go back into that imagination of yourself as that ageless observer of the Old Town several hundred years before. You are doing another walking survey, but this time in 2013. Your route takes you from St Andrew Square west along George Street to Charlotte Square, and then back along Princes Street. You note that people can now stroll through St Andrew Square, and that there is even a coffee shop there. Reaching George Street, you realise that if you were more courageous and agile you could walk from one end of the street to the other right on top of the cars and buses. Parked cars occupy the centre of the wide street, and long lines of buses fill up the lanes. The spacious squares and stately streets have disappeared. The old St Andrew's Church with its one tree is still there, but it is surrounded by commercial enterprises. There are shops selling kitchenware and clothes, books and jewellery and holidays. There are banks and offices dealing with money, insurance, and employment and property. There are hotels and restaurants and coffee shops. Lots of people pass by, but they do not appear to be entering or leaving houses. You are not able to spot any residential properties. You suppose that members of churches in this locale must have to travel some distance on a Sunday. As you reach Charlotte Square you note that St George's is indeed gone, but the square has tents and temporary buildings within it. You learn that it is a book festival. Perhaps Edinburgh is still an intellectual capital. When you turn the corner and approach Princes Street you are glad to see the castle and the houses of Ramsay Gardens still looking down upon the town. The unsightly, smelly Nor Loch is gone, and the space where the loch used to be is beautiful, as are the buildings alongside the Mound. There are people sitting on benches and walking along the paths. That wouldn't have happened in the old days. But Princes Street itself is all torn up. Upon questioning a passer-by, you are informed with the rolling of eyes that it is for the construction of a tram. You feel that you've been there before. You are amazed at how much coming and going there is, how many people seem to be on the move. In all this constant movement of peoples there are few echoes of the ancient past in the Old Town. Even the smoke has disappeared. You study the faces of the people passing by, wondering if somehow you might see the ghosts of Old Provost Drummond, or James Craig or David Hume, or even Alexander Whyte. But no, they do not appear. You complete your survey by walking back to George Street and returning to the church.

The purpose of our surveys, moving from second person to third, is to allow us to obtain some distance from what is over the sweep of many years. Our observer is interested in everything he sees, including the church. Standing in front of this church he reflects on what he has noted. The changes in the city and the society have proved far more radical and far-reaching than he could have anticipated. He tries to isolate the key elements or turning points. Provost George Drummond was certainly right in seeing the pressing need for more human space in the city and in finding the courage to act. James Craig had the creativity and the boldness to respond. The Town Council were acting responsibly in taking the initiative to provide churches for the people, even though they were perhaps misguided in introducing seat-rents. Andrew Mitchell Thomson had the courage to preach against slavery, as did other ministers of the day, underlining the belief that the faith was about expressing moral concern as well as piety. Alexander Whyte, with his humble origins, powerful down-to-earth preaching and effective teaching, proved a strong model for any man or woman. Murdo Ewen Macdonald, with strength and humanity, recognized the need for community and exercised courage in pursuing it. Andrew Wylie swam against the stream by perceiving the need for a radically different ministry by a church in what had changed to an urban setting. Our observer wonders if the church today also recognizes these and other turning points in the life of the city and community. He imagines that it cannot be easy now, in such a secular, acquisitive, and self-absorbed society to proclaim the gospel in a meaningful way. He wonders further if St Andrew's and St George's West, as it is now called on the notice board, with its single tree and its proud and noble history, might still be the active centre of a lively, caring, and intelligent Christian community.

In 1994 in our book *Full on the Eye*: Perspectives on the World, the Church, and the Faith, Ian Gilmour and I wrote the following:
"It is possible then, to project a society largely devoid of the voice of the historic church. A shrunken and introverted

institution will sound increasingly shrill and seen to be marching more and more out of step. As society and the world become increasingly dominated by the media and multinational companies, there will be few voices to challenge prevailing fashions and offer alternative values and views. While it may be argued that the media does at least express a variety of viewpoints, it also displays a united resolve to maintain its power. Without a church strong enough or perceptive enough to express an alternative view of reality, we face the prospect of a secular, homogenised world."[47]

It is somewhat chilling to recognise just how accurate this prediction was, now almost twenty years ago. But in this brief history of St Andrew's and St George's West we have found a number of turning points or learning points that help us to form a stronger and more perceptive church.

Worship is central to the life of the church. John Calvin said that the marks of the true church are the proclamation of the Word and the rightful administration of the sacraments. In practice, this has meant that the proclamation of the Word is central and dominant, with "proclamation" being rather narrowly understood as preaching. In this historical survey we have seen how important preaching has been. The other elements of worship: the sacraments, prayer, readings and music have all taken second place. The thoughtful preparation of these elements of worship has seldom been given the high priority that preaching enjoys. This historic pattern of worship in the Presbyterian Church is so pervasive that any variation in worship is often regarded as unsettling and unwelcome. Even minor changes, like the greeting of people within worship, alarms us.

---

[47] *Full on the Eye, p. 63*

The centrality of preaching enabled the church, or the town council, as the case may be, to institute the idea of seat-rents. Granting members the ownership of seats was not, in the long run, helpful. It may have made sense financially in the early days, but it aided and abetted the idea of worship as theatre. It was indeed the oratory that people went to church to hear. If Edinburgh was genuinely the intellectual capital of the world, then these were undoubtedly intelligent and articulate people who appreciated the oratorical skills of the minister, his literary allusions and the like. Seat-rents meant that the professional and wealthy classes could take advantage of this arrangement, and the poor were excluded. It left a mental heritage about the "ownership of seats" lasting until today, and this has posed perennial problems for a sense of community. It also meant that when other and more compelling forms of entertainment appeared, attendance at worship declined. What is essential for the church today is to shift from the ownership of seats or pews to the ownership of the church's direction of ministry.

Our ideas about the proclamation of the Word come largely from the book of Acts in the New Testament. The apostles were making an appeal for Jesus Christ to Jews and to the Gentile world in the public arenas and the vicinity of the synagogue. But it isn't clear how or whether such a pattern was also employed in the early Christian communities. When these communities met for worship in houses of the saints, was there "preaching" as we know it or was there conversation and teaching along with the common meal? In the seventeenth and eighteenth centuries, the oratorical form through which the Word was presented was clearly very appealing to intelligent people. That is why they paid their seat-rents and filled the pews. That form does not seem so appealing today. The question, daunting as it may be, is: do we actually employ the most appropriate pattern for worship today?

The relevance of the question, however heretical it appears, can be appreciated by noting some other realities. When people go to worship on Sunday, they go with the expectation of being receivers. They sit to pray, listen to the lesson and hear the sermon. They stand or make bodily movements mainly to sing the hymns. The words of the hymns are already formed, as are the words of the lesson and the prayers (for the most part). In relation to the sermon the congregation is passive. The worshippers can only listen, except perhaps to critique it mentally or maybe verbally with their others later. They do not expect to discuss with the preacher or with their fellow-members. Their reception of the Word is a passive experience, although the minister hopes that they will understand it and somehow apply it in the world.

Meanwhile, before Sunday, the minister prepares his sermon diligently, but in his study and in isolation. He also prepares the prayers, and chooses the hymns. On Sunday he leads the worship and delivers the sermon. He does not expect members to criticize the sermon or to offer any substantial discussion about it with him. He would be surprised if anyone wanted to dispute some theological point with him. There is no mechanism for this. The days are gone when the newspaper might print the whole or at least part of his sermon in order to inform the rest of the community. The minister is an active but rather isolated participant in worship and the members are passive, at least in relation to offering any of their own ideas or feelings. There is no obvious exchange of ideas or responses between minister and members or between member and member. As a learning experience, worship is severely limited. Questions cannot be asked and answered, nor can ideas be elaborated or challenged. On the other hand, people can undoubtedly be inspired and perhaps have their minds changed. But the question remains: Does the pattern of worship in our time and society genuinely reflect the purpose of worship as seen in scripture and in the early Christian communities? To be consistent with the Word of God, a form of worship-even a Presbyterian one-must call on more than a long history to justify itself.

Myth. We have seen that at least in the Victorian age worship in the church was far from perfect. Surely the recognition that worship was so lacking and in some respects awful ought in a strange way to be encouraging for us. Assumptions or myths about the past are stubborn and hard to dispel, and it is never possible to live up to what was mythical. In our minds the church of old may always have been full and the worship compelling. We have seen that that wasn't true. There were ministers who attempted to improve the quality of worship and yet the institution often strongly resisted their efforts. The implication is that our worship today, including even the sermon, can be much better than that of yesterday. What if ministers spent as much time in crafting the prayers and choosing the hymns as they do in writing a sermon? What if laymen were much more involved in leading worship, including sharing their own experience and ideas? What if members had more opportunities to discuss the points touched on in the sermon or the important moral issues of the day? Freedom from the myths of the past could be liberating.

Community. How do people think of the church? Is it the larger institution, the collection of individuals on a Sunday morning, or a community? We have seen that at least in one instance, the "sanctuary" or place of worship was regarded merely as the heart of the individual within a collection of individuals. The Disruption, of necessity, forced the focus of ministers and members to be on the larger institution. By challenging patronage the Disruption brought in a positive good. Congregations could now choose their own ministers. But there was still a failure to appreciate that the real sanctuary is the community. **The locus of the means of God's grace is the communion of saints.** The saints have been called by God to offer their various gifts for the building up of the community. Murdo Ewen Macdonald and Andrew Wylie understood this. By failing to understand community and by persisting with a passive pattern of worship we are denying the operation of the grace of God among all the members. If that is true, then the primary work of the minister should be to build up the community, aiming for the priesthood of all believers. The goal of the minister is not to enhance his or her career by means of the institution, but to build up community with the help of the institution. In *Full on the Eye* we spoke about "taking the members off the shelf"[48]. But do we know how to take them off the shelf? Identifying and nurturing the skills that members have and equipping them to use them in the church and the world is vital.

Change. We have seen how change has relentlessly turned our city and world upside down. The world, in 2013, is extremely challenging. The rate of change, especially the technological kind, is ever increasing. Someone has said that

[48] *Full on the Eye, p.86*

technology is like a train coming down a mountain; nothing is going to stop it. It is difficult for anyone over the age of about fifty to keep abreast of this. Our forms of communication have changed profoundly; texting and tweeting offer instant communication, but also dumber communication. We are surrounded by the ubiquitous advert, and our online adventures and communications invade our privacy and track our preferences. Our attempt to escape national indebtedness has led to a widening of the gap between rich and poor. Some of our major intuitions have been exposed as untrustworthy. The news, as it is presented to us, is mostly bad, with large numbers of people apparently seeking revenge, death, and social destruction. Can the church, in such a setting, provide some kind of "sanctuary" which permits us to deal with such change without escaping from the world?

Perception and Courage. In the story of the development of Edinburgh's New Town and our two historic churches we have observed several key people who have perceived the need to some kind of action and had the courage to seek it. Provost Drummond, James Craig, Andrew Mitchell Thomson, Alexander Whyte, Murdo Ewen Macdonald, and Andrew Wylie spring to mind. All of them would have faced resistance to their visions and ideas. In our time, will there be similar individuals who will perceive what is required and have the courage to act on it? Will the members of congregations and the Church of Scotland at large appreciate and encourage such vision and courage?

The Communion of Saints. So, with such a gloomy assessment of the world, what can we say about the church? It is surely an ideal time for the communion of saints who are St Andrew's and St George's, mindful of their immensely valuable history, to create that kind of community in which the world is accurately interpreted in the light of the Word of God, in which every member is encouraged to offer something positive, and in which they receive the grace of God through one another. The One Tree, still standing and alive.

Questions for Further Reflection

This has, of necessity, been a brief theological history of St Andrew's and St George's West. For those who would like to explore more deeply some of the issues raised I include some questions to help.

Try to picture yourself living on the fourth floor in a tenement house in The Old Town:

* *What are the negative features of your life, the things you dislike day by day?*

* *Are there any aspects of life in that setting which might which appeal to you now, in the present day?*

Now picture yourself attending church in St Giles':

* *What might have appealed to you about the worship then?*

* *It is difficult to know, but do you think that the worship of the church has improved since this era?*

* *When people moved from the confines the Old Town to the spaces of the New, what did they gain and what did they lose?*

- *If you were contemplating a move from that tenement flat on the High Street to a new house on George Street, what would be your main concern?*

- *What are the unanticipated consequences, individually and corporately, of renting out seats in the church?*

- *What qualities would have constituted a "popular preacher"? When people filled the church what kind of preaching style were they expecting?*

- *Would Andrew Mitchell Thomson have faced opposition in his denunciation of slavery? If so, from whom?*

- *Do you agree that it was the quality of oratory that drew people to the church rather than the theology?*

- *What difference does it make to us today to hear that the quality of worship in the Victorian Age was so poor?*

- *If you had been a member of St Andrew's or St George's, would you have joined others in walking out to form the Free Church? Why, or why not?*

- *The Disruption stands as a major event in the history of Scotland, yet the organisers of the Great Tapestry of Scotland project in 2012 apparently knew nothing of it. How could this be?*

- *Individualism is a great problem in the world and for the church. Is it possible that the kind of theology we see in Robert Candlish's sermons actually reinforced individualism?*

- *What is appealing about Alexander Whyte's style of preaching?*

- *Why do you think George MacLeod sent his "nasty" letter*

to Murdo Ewen Macdonald?

- *How would you characterise Jesus' kind of ministry? Was he primarily a preacher, a teacher, a miracle-worker or what?*

- *Can you give examples of those ways in which our society is an "I-It" society?*

- *What are the patterns of worship or church life that would find a resonance with people today?*

Appendix: Ministers

St Andrew's

1784   *William Greenfield*#*

1787   *William Moodie*#*

1801   *David Ritchie*#*

1813   *Andrew Grant*#*

1837   *John Bruce**

1843   *Thomas Clark**

1844   *Thomas Jackson Crawford*#*

1857   *John Stuart**

1889   *Hon. Arthur Gordon*

1896   *Peter Hay Hunter**

1908   *George Christie**

1937   *William Erskine Blackburn*

1941   *James Stuart Thomson*

1948   *Donald Davidson**

St Andrew's and St George's

1962   William Cecil Bigwood*

1972   William Andrew Wylie

1986   Andrew R.C. McLellan*#

2003   Roderick D.M. Campbell

* Given the DD (Doctor of Divinity degree)
 # Moderator of the General Assembly

St George's

1814   Andrew Mitchell Thomson*

1831   James Martin

1834   Robert Smith Candlish*#

1843   Robert Horne Stevenson#

1880   Archibald Scott*#

1909   Gavin Land Pagan

1918   Charles William Gray Taylor*#

1951   James Robert Thomson

1956   William Cecil Bigwood

St George's West

1843   Robert Smith Candlish*#

1861   John Oswald Dykes#

1870   Alexander Whyte*#

1896   Hugh Black#

1907   John Kelman#

1921   James Macdougall Black*#

1949   Murdo Ewen Macdonald*

1965   William David Ranald Cattanach*

1985   Robert L. Glover

1998   Peter McDonald

St Andrew's and St George's West

2010   Ian Y. Gilmour

* *Given the DD (Doctor of Divinity degree)*
\# *Moderator of General Assembly or Free General Assembly*

For a more complete list of ministers for all the branches after the Disruption, see Ian Dunlop, The Kirks of Edinburgh

Recollections of a Ministry in Two Churches

By The Very Reverend Andrew McLellan

I walked along Queensferry Street Lane and found Bill Cattanach waiting for me. It was a sunny summer afternoon, he was leaning against the back door, and he was shorter than I expected. For me it was a very important day and one which turned out well: but I remember nothing about it except that first sighting. I suppose we must have talked about St George's West and the expectations placed on a new assistant. I suppose I must have told him something about the year I had spent in New York. I was fresh from studying at Union Seminary, the college for which Rev Hugh Black had left Free St George's sixty years before. But all that conversation is forgotten.

In those days the placing of assistant ministers was less formalised than it is now. It was a hint here, a phone call there – a process more difficult to participate in from the other side of the Atlantic. One minister had written to me to invite me to join him and his congregation: while I was thinking about it (actually on the day I had written to my father for his advice)

I received a letter from Murdo Ewen Macdonald. He had been my professor at Trinity College, Glasgow: and the letter was to suggest that I spend two years at St George's West, which he had left a few years earlier. He had been very kind to me as a student, and I had a high regard and affection for him. Of course I was flattered to receive his suggestion, because I knew how much St George's West meant to him. (The terms of Murdo Ewen's letter – which I still have – are less flattering: "I am fairly certain that not only would you cope, but that you might do a good job". A cautious judgment!) So I agreed to meet Bill Cattanach.

That first conversation with him was important, even though it has made no mark on me. For each of us was sizing up the other. I have no idea what he knew about me, but I knew very little about him (this was a world without internet). At the end of the afternoon we had each to decide if we thought it would work. We did and it did.

I owe a tremendous amount to Bill Cattanach. Most of all because he was patient with me; but also for making me think about what I was doing. I had been a student assistant before – with a very fine Glasgow minister called James Hay Hamilton – but most of that work I had been able to do without thinking about what I was doing. Not so in St George's West and not so with Bill Cattanach. Most of my tasks were traditional assistant minister tasks. There were hospital patients to visit, there was a long list of shut-in members to visit, there was material to prepare for each Sunday (those were the days when most congregations had evening services every Sunday). There was observation: he would take me with him to meetings, to occasional baptism preparation or wedding preparation. And there were funerals. My first two funerals had already taken place. The very first was of a young man in Canada when I had been on a student placement there. He had committed suicide because he owed $300, leaving behind a wife and baby. At St George's West Bill Cattanach took me with him on some pre-funeral visits and some post-funeral visits; and we talked about how to construct the funeral service. There had been a little of that at college, but not much. By the time I left Edinburgh, however, I had conducted several funerals, and I had made the most of the opportunity to talk over everything about them with the supervising minister.

The most difficult part of my two years as assistant minister was work with young people. I followed a very gifted friend, Mike Mair. Mike had been the year ahead of me at Trinity College and was an outstanding student – academically, and in many other ways. Not everyone at St George's West had found him what they wanted, for he could be an unconventional presence: but teenagers (the word was still new then!) loved him. He had begun a new project which was called Action: it was an after-school club. It was an after-school club which often spilled over into the evenings and had many of the well-known marks of successful church youth clubs in the sixties – dances, expeditions, guest talks etc. But the core was the drop-in at the end of the afternoon and young people came in high numbers twice a week.

Mike had an extraordinary rapport with them and a remarkable influence for good. While his magnetic presence was by far the most important element in the leadership, quite a few had emerged from it with real responsibility for the group. Among them all, and especially among those who had been closest to him, the sense of bereavement when Mike left was strong.

For more than a year I did my best. There were some others about my own age who joined in and I would not have coped without them. But it was never the same. I never replaced Mike in the affections of the teenagers; the older ones moved on and others did not come in; and great differences in economic and social background of those who were attending became increasingly divisive. Eventually the project was brought to a close – about which I was sad then and am still (An American friend once joked to me that he was planning a book entitled "Youth Groups I have Failed to Found")!

The two best things to come out of this business were the support of the minister and the loyalty of the congregation. Bill Cattanach stood beside me when there were occasional tensions with some office-bearers as a result of some small damage to property or other awkwardness. So did the St George's West congregation. Even the office-bearers who were landed with clearing up – literally or figuratively – were never annoyed for long and always re-affirmed the importance of the project: and many of the members were quick to praise when things went well. There were reasons for the support of both minister and members. Much of it, of course arose from their Christian faith: both minister and members believed that work among young people was important. And both minister and members believed that people learning how to become ministers should be encouraged and should be treated kindly. But for both there were historical circumstances as well.

If part of the challenge for me was following a high-profile, multi-talented predecessor, then Bill Cattanach could understand. It must have been exciting to be called in 1965 to St George's West in the centre of Edinburgh with over two thousand members; but he too was following a high-profile multi-talented predecessor. Murdo Ewen Macdonald was deservedly a famous preacher with a particular appeal to students. He was also exceptionally funny and could be disarmingly charming. He was bravely committed to several causes not popular in fashionable Edinburgh circles, but they had loved him dearly in St George's West They were still mourning him when I arrived: when they learned that I had been his student in Glasgow the call was usually "Tell us a story about Murdo Ewen!" He was one of those about whom stories abound – some of the best ones he made up himself!

In one way, therefore, Murdo Ewen Macdonald made things easy for me in St George's West. There was a second way. One of the successes of his ministry had been a succession of remarkable assistants who were glad to work with him: so the congregation had learned to create a special place in their hearts. Ian Pitt-Watson, David Smith, David Robertson, George Elliot, Terence McCaughey ... and the peerless Bill Shaw: Murdo Ewen Macdonald had shared his ministry with them and others and the St George's West congregation had come to cherish their assistants.

For Bill Cattanach the Macdonald effect was very different. Bill was certainly a good preacher, a thoughtful preacher, a challenging preacher, a contemporary preacher, but people said he was not the dazzling preacher his predecessor had been. Some of them never quite forgave him for that. Never once – and by the end of two years I had come to know Bill well – never once did I hear him complain of that, or say anything less than warm about "The man from Harris".

When things were not going well for me in Action, the minister had another reason to be sympathetic and supportive. For his experience was that in some ways things were not going well in the congregation and in the Church of Scotland. The numerical decline which had been spreading throughout the whole church since the late fifties had arrived. It hit large congregations most violently, and it hit large congregations which had postponed its arrival, like St George's West, most violently of all. Those whose ministry was at its peak in the sixties and seventies, like Bill Cattanach, perhaps had it hardest. The generation before them knew full churches (they did have to turn people away from evening services in St George's West at one time) and endless streams of young folk. The generation after were already accustomed to small congregations and wondering where the children were. But Bill Cattanach and his generation were learning to be ministers in new circumstances, where no amount of energy and imagination seemed to make much difference.

So there was history behind Bill Cattanach's support of me in the work with young people. And there was history behind the congregation's support also. For years they had backed *Cephas*. *Cephas* had been a successful controversial experiment in what was becoming called "outreach" work with young people with no church connection, some of whom would be in trouble with the police. It was run by Christians on Sunday nights and week nights, and was ecumenical in outlook. *Cephas* was a wonderful pioneer in spirit and in methods, and it changed the life of people. Some of its young

leaders were friends of mine then and spoke movingly about
its impact for good. But by the end of the sixties its day was
coming to an end. In one sense Action was its little sister.
More obviously, its other sister was Cornerstone. This was
work beginning when I was at St George's West, but very
important work it was. Several congregations in the centre of
the city (including St Andrew's and St George's) created a
coffee-house under St John's Church as the home for a new
wave of engagement with a new generation outside the church.
This time the "customer base" was to be slightly older people,
in their twenties and thirties; but again there was the same
imagination and clear-thinking and commitment among
some remarkable people that had been the energy behind
Cephas (indeed several of the Cornerstone pioneers had been
Cephas people; several of them I was to meet again nearly
twenty years later as elders and members in St Andrew's and
St George's). This was an ecumenical project, but St George's
West was in the thick of it. With this history, this congregation
was not likely to be unsupportive of what we were trying to do
with teenagers.

I have dwelt on an experience that for me was less than happy
in St George's West: but they were very few. It was a memorably
happy two years. Perhaps chief among the regular excitements
was Sunday worship. As I have said there were two services,
both traditional in structure, each Sunday. So there were
many opportunities to take part in the conduct of worship.
The pulpit in St George's West was famous (and usually
referred to as "Alexander Whyte's pulpit"). Famous because it
was huge: so big that it contained not a chair but a large couch.
All of the services were conducted from the pulpit, so Sunday
after Sunday Bill Cattanach and I shared a couch in church!

It was a pulpit designed for preaching in a church designed for preaching. It has done me harm in the sense that I have always since then felt imprisoned when contained in a small, narrow pulpit. Alexander Whyte's pulpit was designed for commanding the congregation, and for walking about. So I think it may have done me a little harm in another sense, for it may have encouraged tendencies to a showy, declamatory style of preaching which I do not much like and from which I have grown away. But it was a pulpit which did me a lot of good. It was designed to give the preacher confidence. I needed that and I received that. Noticeably it was a pulpit designed to emphasise the importance of preaching. You could not sit in the church and look at that pulpit and not think that preaching was important; and you certainly could not announce your text from that pulpit and not feel "something tremendous is happening".

I began work when the minister was on holiday: not an ideal arrangement, but one that suited both me and the congregation more than waiting until his return. So at my first Sunday service I was assisting the guest preacher, Professor J S Stewart. His name will be fading with the years, but then he was renowned all across the world. The *American Preaching Magazine*, in its 1999 list of "best preachers of the twentieth century", ranked him number one. He was distantly related to my mother, so he knew me slightly, but I was much in awe of him. I read the wrong lesson! He began his sermon thus: "It was very good that Mr McLellan read some verses from Hebrews chapter three: for that allows us to see the context for my text in chapter four." Then in a couple of sentences he brilliantly made the connection between what I had read and what he had wanted, and dissolved my embarrassment. If I have ever managed to be gracious to the mistakes of those learning how to be ministers it is because of that moment.

That pulpit was designed for preaching in that church which was designed for listening to preaching. From Candlish onwards that congregation revered their ministers, and it was for their preaching they revered them. Alexander Whyte died nearly fifty years before I arrived in Edinburgh, but his name was still spoken in reverential tones. There were many who boasted that they had been baptised by him; and Murdo Ewen Macdonald was very proud when he brought into our classroom a precious possession – Alexander Whyte's annotated Bible, which he had been given by the great man's son. As it happens, I was with Norman Pritchard on his first night as my successor as assistant in St George's West. We were in the homes of one or two members of the congregation; and I chuckled to see him returning from his first night's work clutching Barbour's Life of Alexander Whyte!

For all that it had great ministers and great preachers, it was not merely a minister-centred congregation. There was an earnestness of faith which made a great impression on me: if they had good ministers they were good ministers precisely because they helped them to follow Jesus and to know him. Like most divinity students, I had come to speak of holy things in a casual way: I learned better from the people of St George's West.

In another and more obvious way, they were not merely minister-centred: for they were busy. They were active in all sorts of ways in the two years I was with them. Of course there was the energetic youth work over many years of which I have spoken. There was Mrs T P McDonald's long-running Lunch Club which entertained – in more than one way – high numbers. She always spoke of the minister as "our Captain", and the assistant minister as "the midshipman" (or was it "cabin boy"?). Many years later I was pleased to find myself her daughter's minister in St Andrew's and St George's. There was a lively concern with the Church Overseas with regular visits from missionaries. This commitment to the world church was symbolised by the invitation to the great D. T. Niles from Sri Lanka, President of the World Council of Churches, to lead the Centenary Preaching Festival to mark the centenary of the building during my time there.

Much of this business was traditional: choir, Sunday School, Youth Fellowship. But there was a strong note of innovation as well, as I have mentioned in connection with youth work. The appointment of Ronald Beasley as Community Service Officer of the Council of West End Churches soon after I began as assistant was important for two reasons. It showed that these congregations were prepared not to just say they had an ecumenical commitment but to put money into it. It also showed that these congregations were increasingly determined to serve the community in which they were placed.

That determination led St George's West in particular in two directions. More and more Bill Cattanach began to talk of those who worked in the parish and the responsibility of the congregation to them. This kind of talk was to bear fruit later in the story of St George's West; and was to come to mean a lot to me in the ministry of St Andrew's and St George's many years later. Bill was also keen to make more use of the church building during weekdays: so The Centre was opened – the strength behind it was Lorna Cattanach – as a way of expressing the congregation's service to the community. So when I came to be minister of St Andrew's and St George's the exciting work of the Undercroft was new to me – but some of the imagination and theology which lay behind it was not.

It was often said that St George's West was a generous congregation. That usually referred to high Christian giving; and very ready support for new adventures to help the most needy. But they were generous with themselves as well as with their money. There were invitations to Muirfield, a couple of spells in holiday cottages, unending encouragement, and remarkable tolerance. It was very daunting to preach week in and week out to the judges and professors in the pews there. Professor Cheyne, for example, had an unparalleled reputation as a church historian. Some of the stuff in my sermons must have made him cringe: but every Sunday, without exception, he said something generous. Sunday lunch at the manse, where I was often to be found, was great fun. There was Betty McKay, the church secretary, who looked after me; and there was Mrs Park. Mrs Park had been church secretary for years, and easily a match for Murdo Ewen and Bill Shaw. She was a rare combination of simple goodness and sharp quick-wittedness. She took me into her home for weeks when I was homeless and it was never dull. I visited her when she was well over ninety and found her beaming. "One of my life-long friends is about to be married: and she has asked me to be her bridesmaid"!

St George's West was born in the Disruption of 1843, when Rev Robert Candlish led members of his congregation out of the great Charlotte Square St George's Church to find a new home. That Charlotte Square St George's was to unite with its neighbour in George Street in 1964 to form St Andrew's and St George's. For years there was a gulf fixed between the two St George's congregations. There is a story about Alexander Whyte which is difficult to believe, but it appears in his biography. The renowned minister of St George's in Charlotte Square, Dr Archibald Scott, had invited Whyte to speak at a meeting in the very church from which Robert Candlish departed in 1843. A Mr Clarke "records how, as they approached together the broad flight of steps leading up to the lofty columns of the portico, his companion withdrew the arm linked in his own and shrank back with a troubled look, while the words broke from him: 'I cannot do it: I cannot do it'. Mr Clarke looked inquiringly, and Dr Whyte added: 'You do not understand; but I cannot do it: no minister of Free St George's has gone up those steps since Dr Candlish came down them in 1843.'" The depth of feeling aroused by the Disruption even many years after is now difficult to grasp. The fine building of St George's was to close in 1964; but its name and congregation lived on. What would Dr. Whyte have thought at the time? For in that year the one who had been ordained a minister in the very building Whyte had made famous as Free St George's would become the first minister of the newly united St Andrew's and St George's!

I know what I thought of it: I was very excited. In the spring of 1986 I entered a newspaper competition and won a prize. The prize was a copy of a novel called *The Awakening of George Darroch*, about a minister caught up in the storms of the Disruption. The front cover has a picture of St Andrew's Church, in Edinburgh's George Street, where the Disruption took place. On the day that prize and that picture popped through our letter-box, the Secretary of the St Andrew's and

St George's Vacancy committee, Eric Donaldson, telephoned me with the invitation to become minister at that very church.

I was very excited and did not find it difficult to accept. Not that we had been keen to leave the fine congregation in Stirling and the fine town of Stirling where we were happy. But St Andrew's and St George's seemed special. Partly it was because of publicity I had seen about the bicentenary of the building. There had been a television programme about the exciting new work being done on the building and about the exciting work being done in the building and from the building. There had been a piece in *Life and Work* in which a member of the congregation – it was Marjory McNeill – had spoken about "this wonderful church".

I had been in the church once before (I think for a Donald Swann concert, although I remember nothing about it). But I was not prepared for the joy of seeing it soon after its bicentenary refurbishment. I thought it then, and think it still, the loveliest church building in Scotland. That sense of joy in the building was a wonderful gift to me. Often in the next sixteen years I would find myself sitting on top of the steps leading up to the communion table gazing around and marvelling at the privilege of being minister in these surroundings. In his book *The Making of Classical Edinburgh*, A. J. Youngson was not exaggerating when he called it a minor masterpiece. I always knew, however, that the St Andrew's and St George's building did not have the same magical effect on everyone. Soon after I was called there I had a conversation with a senior academic theologian, whom I had known all my life and whose opinions mattered to me. "Why would you want," he asked me, "to be a minister in an eighteenth century drawing-room?"!

There was a historical curiosity in moving from Viewfield Church in Stirling to St Andrew's and St George's. Viewfield Church sometimes calls itself Viewfield Erskine, tracing its story back to Ebenezer Erskine, the leader of the Original Secession. This was a division in the church in 1733 about patronage and the right of appointment of ministers, a story with many similarities to the Disruption: a division only healed when United Presbyterian elements in the United Free Church were made one with the Church of Scotland in 1929. So in 1983, on the 250th anniversary of the Secession, I was minister of a congregation which marked its place in the history of the first great separation in the Church of Scotland; and in 1993, on the 150th anniversary of the Disruption, I was minister in a congregation which marked its place in the story of the second such separation.

In April 1986 I arrived in a beautiful building on an exceptional site with a dramatic history. None of these things mattered as much, however, as the springing up of new life in the congregation which had been the mark of the ministry of my predecessor, Andrew Wylie. During his years St Andrew's and St George's had grown from a congregation unsure of its identity in a changing world to one which had rediscovered its role as the parish church for the community of the centre of the city and had rediscovered energy and imagination and commitment in the process. Andrew Wylie's ministry was remarkably creative: when he left all sorts of doors were opening. It was not, and would not become, a large congregation, but life and liveliness are not always measured in numbers. Much of the energy of St Andrew's and St

George's when I was there had its roots in the inspiration of Andrew Wylie.

We tried to do three things well: variety in worship, mission and service to the parish, commitment to the poor, and commitment to the arts. These things were in the Congregational Plan which the Kirk Session produced at the end of the eighties, and were objectives often spoken about. Of course there were many of the marks of congregational life which all congregations have in greater or less degree. But the three objectives noted above related specifically to the situation of St Andrew's and St George's and the particular commitments of its members.

Variety of worship did not mean that every Sunday was different: rather it meant that on any Sunday there would be acts of worship which were different from each other. It was not hoped that every Sunday worshippers would be surprised by some new experience: but that every Sunday people with different backgrounds and experiences and needs would find something helpful for their worship. This thinking was explicitly designed with visitors in mind. Surely a church in one of the great streets at the centre of Scotland's capital city, next door to a large hotel, could expect numbers of visitors, and visitors from all over the world? The reality never quite met the hopes; almost every Sunday there would be visitors, but never were there countless visitors.

The Sunday structure did not change from that established when I arrived. There were three services each Sunday. The first was a communion service. So the congregation had recovered the ancient practice of weekly communion: one of very few congregations in the Church of Scotland to do so. The weekly communion service never became the main service (at that service there was eventually communion monthly) and the numbers were small enough to allow those present to stand around the communion table to share bread and wine. There was a set liturgy in which all participated, no music and a brief address.

George MacLeod came to this service most Sundays. He had been one of the great figures in the Scottish church, and indeed in the life of Scotland; and he was an unforgettable preacher. As an old man his powers began to fail, but it was still an awe-inspiring and intimidating experience to preach to the great man. Always he would say the same thing as he left the church: "Thank you very much – never heard a word"! He was long remembered in St Andrew's and St George's after an occasion at the main service when a number of ministers and deacons who were associated with the congregation took part. He was nearing the end of his life and it was not easy to work out with him what he would say. We agreed on a reflection on some verses from Romans – the sort of thing that he could thrill you with. These days were the height of Mrs Thatcher's power, and she was as divisive a force in the congregation as she was in the country (although no-one had any doubt of my aversion to much of what she stood for). When his moment came George MacLeod made no reference to Romans but simply proclaimed "Jesus said, 'Love your enemies'. Mrs Thatcher is our enemy. We must love her". No-one remembered anything else said that day!

The second service had the unimaginative name of "The 9.45 service". At its best this was all-age worship. It was certainly the service to which most of the children in the church came. If there was any innovative worship material, making use of the talents of all the members in the congregation's worship it was most likely to be found at 9.45. If there was any serious study of the Bible and the life of the world going on in the congregation on a regular basis it was most likely to be found at 9.45. And it was at 9.45 that the most obvious evidence of people being bound together into community could be seen. The services could be repetitive, the material used for study with children and with adults varied in quality, not everyone found the increased intimacy of small groups to their liking, and it did not generate an easy progression for children into others forms of church life as they grew older. But at its best it was a really exciting weekly celebration: and for years provided our family with the spiritual home we needed.

The main service was traditional in shape: I found it had a "high church" flavour and that did not change. There was a robed choir, an active and responsive liturgy, much of the service conducted from prayer desks or the communion table, and regular use of the lectionary. There was an eager expectation of preaching, and I loved preaching from that pulpit. While it was not nearly as dominating as the one I had known as an assistant in St George's West, it fitted its own very different building perfectly and allowed the balance of closeness and authority which suited me well. I was always pleased when visiting preachers told me how helpful they found the pulpit for preaching, and they told me that often.

All of the congregations which made up St Andrew's and St George's had had outstanding ministers and outstanding preachers. The two names I heard most often were Donald

Davidson and C.W.G. Taylor. Both of them, it seemed, had been adored by their respective congregations, the one in St Andrew's and the other in St George's. Dr Davidson's name lived on both in one of the rooms of the building which was named after him, and in the presence of his son, Kemp Davidson, in the congregation. I had seen him often in the General Assembly where he was Procurator, and he was very formidable. By the time I became his minister he was a judge and it was easy to be in awe of him. But Lord Davidson never forgot he was the son of a minister and was without fail (even when he did not agree with me) helpful, supportive and encouraging. C.W.G. Taylor had been Moderator of the General Assembly in 1942. Soon after I began in St Andrew's and St George's I was visiting an old woman for the first time. Conversation was not proving easy and my eyes lighted on a photograph of C.W.G. Taylor in full Moderatorial gear. "I see Dr. Taylor's picture", I ventured. "Did you know him well?" "Yes indeed" she replied. "He was a real minister".

Three forms of worship every Sunday; and worship every day. We never found the secret for making daily worship the centre of the congregation's life, but day after day, year after year St Andrew's and St George's worshipped God, no matter how many were present. Daily worship grew out of the practice of Tuesday lunch-time communion services held in the Undercroft, a practice which was gladly continued. The plan was to make worship available for all who passed through, members, members of other congregations, visitors, wanderers. Tuesday communions were always the best attended of the week-day services: but there was an important sign in every-day worship that every day belongs to God. Even when the numbers were small, every day was being hallowed by prayer, people were being prayed for, and the world was not forgotten.

The Undercroft was one of the main thrusts of the outreach of the congregation to its parish, its mission and service to the community around. Traditionally, congregations of the Church of Scotland understood their parish responsibilities as responsibilities to those who lived in their parishes. This made little sense in St Andrew's and St George's, where the number of residents in the parish was small. But what if the parish church might discover a sense of care and responsibility for those who work in its parish? For St Andrew's and St George's the number then becomes huge, because of all the shops and offices which line Princes Street and Charlotte Square, Rose Street and St Andrew Square. This discovery was the great and lasting contribution of Andrew Wylie.

The Undercroft was a lounge under the church in which simple lunches were served to anyone who came in: but the purpose was to provide a service to workers in the parish. Lunch was prepared and served by volunteers, and the team of volunteers numbered about eighty. So it was an important part of the life, not merely of the building and the congregation, but also of many of its members. Today a church café is a familiar idea, but the Undercroft in its hey-day was pioneering and we were proud of it.

It was not merely about soup. Welcome and a listening ear were integral to the thinking about what a church should be offering to busy workers in their lunch times: many of the volunteers were not good at clearing the dishes but splendid at knowing when a few minutes of company could be critical (although the ones who were good at clearing dishes were equally necessary). There was always a minister present: all city-centre ministers will recognise the great variety of conversations and needs which every lunch-time produced: and also the sad familiarity of many of the conversations and needs. There was worship every day. And there were regular attempts at speakers and events and sometimes a little music. As I look back over sixteen years I have to concede that some of these attempts were not as successful as they deserved to be!

The other thrust of the outreach of the congregation to its parish was the appointment of another minister to be chaplain to the shops and offices of the city centre. The succession of people who held this office before and during my time is a succession of extraordinarily gifted people: Robert Mathers, Mary Levison, Richard Baxter, Ken Pattison, Tony Bryer. Tony Bryer's appointment made history, since he was a priest of the Church of England working in a congregation of the Church of Scotland and under the authority of its minister and Kirk Session. I invited the Moderator and Clerk of Edinburgh Presbytery and the Episcopal Bishop of Edinburgh to think with me how that would work; and we devised an "induction service" which may not have met every demand of the law of the churches involved, but firmly established Tony Bryer as a ground-breaking ecumenical experiment. The measure of the success of this experiment is his reappointment to a similar position with Edinburgh city centre congregations ten years after he left St Andrew's and St George's for a vicarage in England.

The plan was to visit many of the places of work in the parish on a regular basis and develop a real chaplaincy in those where there was most interest. It might involve lunch at the office canteen, or moving slowly across a shop floor, or keeping an appointment with a member of staff wanting to talk about a wedding. One of the ministers appointed to this work described it as "holy floor-walking and evangelical eating"! Much of it may not have gone deep; and some of it was bound to remain private. But the cumulative result of years of committed mission and service from the parish church was an respect and affection and loyalty towards St Andrew's and St George's from much of the business and retail community of Edinburgh.

Richard Baxter told me a story which became for me a parable of one of the roles of the church in the secular city. A woman approached him for help. She was involved in a dispute with her employer and had to appear at a disciplinary hearing. She was allowed to bring a supporter and asked Richard, her workplace chaplain, to be at her side. He suggested to her that he knew nothing of employment law and that he did not really know her very well. "I know that, Mr Baxter", she said. "But the thing is that I know I can trust you". So he agreed to help her. He then went to the managing director of the firm to tell him what he had agreed to do, so that there would be nothing covert about his action. "I'm very pleased to hear it, Mr Baxter", he said. "For I know I can trust you". There is something precious there: a Christian minister being told that he is trusted by both sides in an industrial dispute.

Variety in worship, mission and service to the parish outside: the third motivation for much of the life of St Andrew's and St

George's has been the commitment of the congregation to the poor and to Christian Aid in particular. This led to my first real decision as minister. Could the church building, the sanctuary itself, be used for a book sale? For a few years a book sale for the sake of the world's poor had been growing in success: it was now too big, and the only space which would be large enough to contain it as it continued to grow would be inside the church itself. There was real opposition: but the sale moved inside the church. Soon it grew to fill every available inch inside and out: and the old arguments were forgotten.

The Christian Aid Sale was easily the best known part of the life of St Andrew's and St George's: in Edinburgh and Scotland and far-off places. Each year the arrival of a core helper from the USA is a sign that final preparations for the great event have begun. It was very familiar to introduce myself as the minister of St Andrew's and St George's and hear the response "Ah! The Book Sale". So astonishing are the statistics that I tried to persuade the Guinness Book of Records to call it The Biggest Book Sale in the World. That I failed to persuade them does not mean it was not true!

It was difficult to be a member of St Andrew's and St George's and not be involved. George Hunt was well into his 90s (he was thrilled to tell me that his grandson had just become a grandfather) and did not walk well: what better post for him then than Head of Security? As the sale grew it grew beyond the resources of the congregation. So from its early days it became an ecumenical venture; and indeed attracted many helpers over the years with little church connection.

Among the delights sold to support Christian Aid, the churches in action with the world's poor, I remember Tony Blair's School *Report Card* from his days in Edinburgh (top in Drama for accuracy, appreciation and atmosphere). I remember another politician visiting. Donald Dewar was a collector of antiquarian books and arrived one day when he was Secretary of State for Scotland. He picked up a book he recognised, called it "very fine" and said, "I hope you are not giving this away cheaply. You should get £50 or £60 for it." Was I pleased to open it and discover it marked £55?!

It was the biggest individual effort in the country by one congregation for Christian Aid. Those behind its annual planning and delivery needed remarkable amounts of energy and brains and commitment: without energy and brains and commitment it would have failed. For me it was inspirational to think that not a penny was for our own use: every penny given away in the cause of the poorest people in the world. The Sale was already famous before I reached Edinburgh. At that time I remember a former Moderator of the General Assembly reflecting with me that the amount raised was magnificent; but then he went on "It is a pity it's not money raised for the church". Neither then nor later did I agree with him.

The task of moving over 100,000 books in and out of the church on a daily basis soon outgrew the resources of the congregation. A member of the congregation made a suggestion. "I work in Edinburgh Prison. I know where there are plenty of strong young men who would be thrilled to have the opportunity to carry heavy boxes of books." So we asked prisoners for help. It was a decisive moment in at least three ways. It made the physical management of the sale possible. It began a relationship between St Andrew's and St George's and prisoners which was important on different levels. And it was to be a key factor in my later appointment as HM Chief Inspector of Prisons for Scotland. It began not by asking what we could do to help prisoners, but by asking prisoners to help us.

Prisoners became familiar figures around the church, and not just at Christian Aid time. St Andrew's and St George's was named a placement for prisoners being prepared for release. At various times they were serving in the Undercroft, working in the kitchen, carrying out cleaning duties, and so on. There were hesitations: but in general I was surprised at the enthusiasm with which the congregation took on the project. I know that it had a significant effect on the lives of some (although not all) of the prisoners. And I know that it had a significant effect on the congregation. The engagement was more and more seen as part of our Christian purpose. Many members found their views changing. It was one thing to have general opinions about crime and punishment: and quite another when Tom and Jack and David became people you knew and people whose stories you knew.

During the sixteen years of my ministry, St Andrew's and St George's stayed close to these marks of our life: variety in worship, mission and service to the parish, commitment to the poor. There was much else that we cared about as well: the things which are central to the life of any happy congregation. Many people fulfilled great commitment in the nurture of children and young people, in the care of the elderly and bereaved, in the music of the congregation. Christian giving was consistently high. There were Christmas Suppers and congregational outings and support for all sorts of other organisations (The remarkable charity *Edinburgh Direct Aid* was born in the home of a St Andrew's and St George's elder and set off on its first aid convoy to Bosnia from George Street with the whole congregation on a Sunday morning lining the pavement, cheering and singing the 121st psalm).

There were at least two other ways in which we sought to be the church for the city. One was St Andrew's and St George's at Festival Time. The "Herald" called St Andrew's and St George's "the premier chamber music venue on the Fringe." Over the years the style of the Festival Fringe (and occasional official Festival) productions changed: chamber music emerged as a leading element partly because of the style of the building and partly because of the interests of those with responsibility for the church's programme. Sometimes there was support for young Fringe performers, and those with special needs; sometimes there were explicitly Christian groups; there was country dancing and Clarsach music; and there were performers from all over the world.

Some performers became firm favourites over the years. Don Kawash came several times from the United States; he was a friend of Lindsay Sinclair, the Director of Music. His reputation arrived before him, for he was a three-time winner of the All-America Ragtime Piano competition. By profession Don was a teacher of history, and it was with a history teacher's gift that he made the story of the growth of piano music in America's black community live. People enjoyed the stories, and they loved the music. I had heard Vivien Liu sing at a service in the Church of Scotland church in Geneva, and immediately invited her to Edinburgh and to St Andrew's and St George's at Festival Time. She was an economist with the World Trade Organisation with a beautiful soprano voice and a large classical repertoire. From every concert she sang in the church over several years she donated the proceeds to Christian Aid. Years later she came to stay with us on her honeymoon – with her Church of Scotland minister husband.

Another attempt to engage with the people of the whole city of Edinburgh was through "Night School". For several winters a series of "classes" would be provided offering serious education of serious themes of Christian history and theology (although they were not as ambitious as the famous "classes" which Alexander Whyte had conducted in Free St George's a century before). There were reading lists and proper "homework", but no exams! Probably half of those who came had a connection with St Andrew's and St George's; and half came from outside. Many of those who arrived simply for the courses were members of no church.

The most important and the most successful course ran in the winter of 2001-2, and was a direct response to the events of September 11, 2001. Suddenly everyone was talking about Islam. Far from being an obscure aspect of comparative religion, Islam became the object of suspicion and fear in daily conversation and nightly television broadcasts. We advertised widely a course which was to give an account of what Islam was and how Christians might think about it. Hundreds came. The aim was to overcome fear, so as well as attending lectures and watching videos and reading books people were expected to have conversations with Muslim citizens of Edinburgh. Very many people told me it was the first time they had had any kind of serious conversation with their local shopkeeper. I was very pleased, not that Muslims came to these evenings, for I had expected that, but that most of them came back and back again. The high point was a visit to the local mosque made by dozens of course participants. In the aftermath of 9/11 this was a meaningful gesture which was a source of excitement both in church and in mosque (as was the return visit some months later). The whole adventure fitted so well the St Andrew's and St George's conviction that Christianity is at its best when it is exploratory, challenged, challenging and well-informed.

It is no accident that this remembering of St George's West and of St Andrew's and St George's should end with the echoes of one in the life of the other a century later. For all Alexander Whyte's anxiety about ascending the steps of St George's, my experiences in both congregations have been similar. I found old friends in St Andrew's and St George's whom I had first met in ecumenical company in St George's West. Many others had friendships and family relationships and professional associations which spanned the two congregations. One such family story was of Joseph Bell. He has an assured place in literary history. The story goes that his unusual powers of deduction displayed in the medical laboratory so impressed his young student, Arthur Conan Doyle, that Sherlock Holmes was modelled on him. Dr Bell was an elder in Free St George's; he was Alexander Whyte's doctor and one of his most intimate friends. Seventy years after his death I ordained his direct descendant as an elder in St Andrew's and St George's.

Several parallels could be drawn between the two congregations. Both were proud of their history; both were generous with their money and their compassion for others. Each congregation grew in its mission and service to the parish around it: each sought the highest standards of worship in the context of an open, enquiring faith. But for me the closeness between the two congregations is more personal. I was very happy in both. St George's West knew how to care for its assistants and St Andrew's and St George's knew how to care for its ministers. Murdo Ewen Macdonald called the kindness of St George's West to him "a miracle of grace". I know what he meant – twice over.